WESTERN GREAT LAKES LIGHTHOUSES

BY BRUCE ROBERTS *and* RAY JONES

Southern Lighthouses
Chesapeake Bay to the Gulf of Mexico

Northern Lighthouses
New Brunswick to the Jersey Shore

Western Lighthouses
Olympic Peninsula to San Diego

Eastern Great Lakes Lighthouses
Ontario, Erie, and Huron

Western Great Lakes Lighthouses
Michigan and Superior

WESTERN
Great Lakes
LIGHTHOUSES

MICHIGAN *and* SUPERIOR

PHOTOGRAPHS *by* BRUCE ROBERTS
TEXT *by* RAY JONES

A Voyager Book

The
Globe
Pequot
Press

Old Saybrook, Connecticut

A Fresnel lens consists of separate, hand-polished prisms fitted into a metal frame. The prisms gather light, focusing it into a concentrated beam. Invented by French physicist Augustin Fresnel in 1822, a Fresnel would be manufactured in Paris, shipped across the Atlantic in pieces, and painstakingly reassembled inside a lantern room. Fresnels came in a variety of sizes, or "orders," ranging from sixth-order (about seventeen inches high and a foot wide) to first-order (as much as ten feet high and six feet wide). This third-order Fresnel still shines from the lantern room of the Devils Island Lighthouse in Wisconsin's Apostle Islands.

All photographs, unless otherwise credited, are by Bruce Roberts.
Editorial research by Cheryl Shelton-Roberts
Book design by Nancy Freeborn

Library of Congress Cataloging-in-Publication Data
Roberts, Bruce.
    Western Great Lakes lighthouses : Michigan and Superior / photographs by Bruce Roberts ; text by Ray Jones.
      p. cm. — (The lighthouses series)
    Includes bibliographical references and index.
    ISBN 1-56440-954-6
    1. Lighthouses—Great Lakes—History. I. Jones, Ray. II. Title. III. Series: Lighthouse series (Old Saybrook, Conn.)
VK1023.3.R6324 1996
387.1'55'0977—dc20
                                        95-53718
                                          CIP

Printed in Quebec, Canada
First Edition / Second Printing

To MARION *and* WES ROBERTS

—*Bruce Roberts*

Perched on a cliff above Lake Superior, the world's largest and stormiest expanse of fresh water, the famed Split Rock Lighthouse symbolizes the struggles of humankind against the leviathan forces of nature. Located near the end of the St. Lawrence Seaway, more than 2,300 navigable miles from the salt waters of the Atlantic, Split Rock ranks among the most spectacular and best known of all inland lighthouses.

ACKNOWLEDGMENTS

When my wife, Cheryl, and I started out photographing lighthouses on Lakes Superior and Michigan, we had no idea how many people would help us along the way. We know we can't mention everyone (there were so many), but here are some special people. First is Randall Childerhose of the Canadian Coast Guard at Parry Sound. An excellent photographer, he provided us with the photograph of Caribou Island Lighthouse. Ned and Shelagh Basher of the Rossport Inn at Rossport, Ontario, provided wonderful information about the Battle Island Lighthouse and the story of the sinking nearby of the yacht *Gunilda*. The mast from the *Gunilda* is now the inn flagpole, and there are other artifacts inside along with good food and accommodations. Farther south on the American side of the lake, Marsha Hamilton at the State Historic Park at Mackinaw City, Michigan, dug out historical information about the lighthouse there, which has been replaced by the bridge. Bill Herd of the Sleeping Bear Dunes National Lakeshore on South Manitou Island provided the picture of the lighthouse when we ran out of time.

We never will forget the Driftwood Ice Cream Parlor and Eatery at Eagle Harbor, Michigan, where Kris Beddigs make special lighthouse ice-cream sundaes. We walked in just as she was closing, about nine in the evening, and she stayed open and cooked pasties (meat-and-vegetable minipies) for a weary photographer and book researcher that saved the day. Gratitude also goes to the Big Bay Lighthouse B&B owners for their hospitality. While there, we were treated to the best nature has to offer: an evening storm with spectacular lightning and resoundings of thunder, a rainbow, and, finally, the peaceful close of a Lake Superior sunset.

Lee Radzak, the site manager at Split Rock Lighthouse, put on his lighthouse keeper's uniform and turned on the big third-order Fresnel lens for my camera. Dick Moehl, president of the Great Lakes Lighthouse Keepers Association, and Jack Edwards, also of GLLKA, helped us get out to St. Helene Island to photograph the restored lighthouse. Dave Snyder, National Park Service historian of the Apostle Islands National Lakeshore, restored our faith in the national park system. Fran Plantske, a lighthouse child who lived in the Apostles, gave us wonderful stories. Ken Black of the Shore Museum in Rockland, Maine, sent us photocopies of the Old Lighthouse Service bulletins. Gary Soule, curator of the Door County Maritime Museum in Sturgeon Bay, Wisconsin, provided information about the Door County lighthouses. Ann Hoge, a lighthouse keeper's daughter, sent us information on lighthouses from Copper Harbor to Passage Island, where she grew up.

Back in Washington, D.C., Dr. Robert M. Browning, historian of the United States Coast Guard, was there with a helping hand. Candace Clifford of the National Park Service Maritime Initiative compiled facts on American lighthouses. James Cassedy of the National Archives, Suitland Reference Division, found our lost notes and request for photocopies. James W. Claflin of Kenrick A. Claflin & Son, dealers in nautical antiques in Northborough, Massachusetts, took in earnest our requests for early lighthouse records.

And thanks to my wife, Cheryl, for putting up with long drives, late hours; for keeping notes that I would have lost; for carrying camera equipment up and down countless steps to lighthouses; and for smiles at the end of exhausting days.

—*Bruce Roberts*

Special thanks to Arthur Layton for his time and expertise in helping obtain information for the expansive area covered by this book.

—*Ray Jones*

CONTENTS

Wearing a circa-1910 Lighthouse Service uniform, site manager Lee Radzak of the state park system gazes out onto Lake Superior from the lantern room of Minnesota's famous Split Rock Lighthouse. No longer used as a navigational aid, the station's enormous clamshell lens once guided shipping through the world's largest freshwater lake. Today it inspires awe in thousands of summer visitors.

INTRODUCTION

Each November 10 Lee Radzak performs a ritual almost as old as civilization itself: lighting the lamp of a lighthouse. With darkness sweeping in from the east over the broad expanses of Lake Superior, Radzak sets about the evening chores that, in one form or another, have occupied lighthouse keepers since the time of the ancient Egyptians. Climbing the thirty-two-step spiral staircase of Minnesota's famed Split Rock Lighthouse, where he is resident keeper and historian, he checks the machinery. It all appears in proper working order. Laboriously, he raises the 250-pound weights that power the turn-of-the-century clockwork mechanism and rotate the light's heavy glass lens.

Radzak is meticulous in every detail of his task. He must take great care, partly because, for all its massiveness—the chandelierlike lens assembly weighs more than six tons—the operating parts of a lighthouse are quite delicate and easily damaged. But Radzak's precision reaches beyond mere prudence. It is, in fact, his way of honoring earlier Split Rock Lighthouse keepers, who took their work no less seriously than he.

Finally, Radzak throws the switch that brings the Split Rock Light to life. The big, French-made Fresnel lens brightens and begins to turn, flinging bright flashes out into the night at regularly spaced intervals. This is always a fine moment for Radzak, who takes pride in keeping alive an ages-old professional tradition.

For as long as ships have sailed the Earth's mighty lakes, seas, and oceans, men and women have struggled to keep lights burning on the shore and to guide mariners home from the deep. Throughout history sailors have anxiously scanned the dark horizon, searching for a light to help them find a safe harbor or avoid dangerous obstacles. Lake Superior's sailors, however, no longer look to Split Rock for guidance in the night. Its lighthouse has been blacked out on most nights since 1969, when the U.S. Coast Guard declared the light obsolete and put it out of service. Radio beacons, radar, and even satellites now do the work once done by the lighthouse and its keepers.

Coast Guard officials are anxious to keep the old lighthouse in the dark. During its annual ceremonial lightings, they require Radzak to limit its power sharply and adjust the beam of its huge lens out of focus with the horizon. Otherwise, seeing a light where there usually is none, the captains and navigators of ships out on the lake might be confused.

Although it serves no practical purpose, Radzak persists in firing up the Split Rock Lighthouse every November 10. The date is a significant one for him and for other lovers of lake lore and exciting sea stories. The lighting is a tribute to the brave captain and crew of one of the most widely remembered ships ever to sail the "inland seas," also known as the Great Lakes. The ship and its crew of twenty-nine men met a tragic and mysterious end on November 10, 1975.

THE SAGA *of the* EDMUND FITZGERALD

Anyone in America within hearing of a radio during the last decade is sure to have heard Gordon Lightfoot's "Ballad of the *Edmund Fitzgerald*." The song tells the true story of an enormous ship that sailed into the teeth of a prodigious storm on Lake Superior and, without warning or explanation, simply disappeared.

Most song lyrics worthy of serious attention have meaning on several levels, and this is certainly the case with Lightfoot's haunting ballad. But surely chief among its themes is that nature is unconquerable. The song reminds us that, even in this prideful technological age of instant satellite communication, radar navigation, and ships' bridges banked high with electronic hardware, human beings in general and sailors in particular are still at the mercy of the elements.

The incident described in the ballad took place only recently. This was no treasure ship wrecked along the Spanish Main four centuries ago, no early twentieth-century maritime disappearance attributed perhaps to latter-day pirates. No, Lightfoot's song is about a modern ship, a giant freighter 729 feet in length and displacing upward of 40,000 tons of water when fully loaded with iron ore. And the *Edmund Fitzgerald* vanished not from the mid-Pacific, the bowels of the Indian Ocean, or the storm-wracked Caribbean, but from the middle of a lake.

Here is the true story of the *Edmund Fitzgerald,* or as much of it as is known. When launched at River Rouge, Michigan, on a bright June day in 1958, she was the world's largest freshwater freighter. Named for a successful Milwaukee banker, she was as proud a ship as was ever lapped by lake water. Some called her the "Queen of the lakes," while others knew her as the "King." Her long, clean lines made her a fond and familiar sight to residents of port cities and towns from Toledo to Duluth. She became such a star that a Detroit newspaper ran a regular column to keep readers informed of her activities.

Indeed, the "Big Fitz"—the affectionate nickname used by her crew—was quite a ship. Able to carry more than 25,000 tons of iron ore, she had a muscular, 7,000-horsepower steam turbine that could whisk the big ship and her enormous cargo along at better than sixteen miles per hour. From 1958 onward, year after year, she set one record after another for carrying bulk freight. Usually the records she broke were her own. Her successes swelled the breasts of her captain and crew with pride and lined her owners' pockets with fat profits. By the time the *Edmund Fitzgerald* steamed out of Duluth, Minnesota, on the afternoon of Sunday, November 9, 1975, she had plied the shipping channels of the Great Lakes for more than seventeen years. She was still in her prime, by lake standards, and just as solid and capable as the day she was launched.

On this trip her holds were filled to the brim with 26,013 tons of taconite, marble-sized pellets of milled iron ore. Often she carried passengers as well as cargo and had two luxury staterooms and a comfortable lounge to accommodate them. But the Great Lakes are notorious for the great, dark, howling storms that churn their waters in the month of November. Potential lake passengers are wary of the month, as well they should be, and choose to travel shipboard earlier in the year. So the *Fitzgerald* left Duluth carrying only the taconite and twenty-nine lake sailors.

Most of the crew were Midwesterners; fourteen of them were from Ohio and eight from Wisconsin. A few came from as far away as Florida or California. All were seasoned sailors, and older members of the crew especially had weathered many a raging Lake Superior gale. The men ranged from their midtwenties to near retirement age. At sixty-two, Captain Ernest McSorley was among the oldest.

Signing on as a deckhand aboard a seagoing freighter at age eighteen, McSorley had made the merchant marine his livelihood and his life. Transferring to the lakes, the young sailor moved steadily up the chain of command, eventually becoming master of his own ship—the youngest master, in fact, on the Great Lakes. By November 1975 McSorley had been captain of the *Edmund Fitzgerald* for many years.

According to McSorley's friends, the "Big Fitz" was, after his wife and family in Toledo, the love of his life. He rarely took time off, even when he was ill, and spent up to ten months a year aboard his ship. He knew her every quirk and idiosyncrasy—her tendency to roll queasily or to bend and spring like a rebounding diving board in high waves. But McSorley had resolute faith in the ability of the *Fitzgerald* to weather a storm—even a Lake Superior storm in November. Perhaps that is why, when Monday, November 10, dawned, bringing gale warnings and fierce winds, McSorley kept the *Fitzgerald*'s bow pointed down-lake toward Whitefish Point and Sault Ste. Marie.

Old foghorns are silhouetted against storm clouds blowing in at the Split Rock Lighthouse on Lake Superior. Since high levels of iron within the surrounding rocks of the lakeshore often caused unusual magnetic readings in navigational equipment, the foghorns were considered vital when visibility was impaired by "heavy weather."

The *Arthur M. Anderson,* a U.S. Steel ore carrier under the command of Captain J. B. Cooper, had left Duluth not long after the *Fitzgerald.* When the weather turned unexpectedly sour, McSorley made radio contact with Cooper, whose ship trailed his own by about ten miles. The two captains agreed to stay in close communication and decided jointly that their ships would slip out of the traditional freighter channel along the lake's southern shores. Instead, they would steer for the northeast, where the leeward shore might provide some protection from the weather. They would soon discover, however, that there was no shelter from this storm. By midday on the 10th, the *Fitzgerald* and *Anderson* were battling seventy-mile-per-hour winds and thirty-foot waves.

By the middle of the afternoon, the *Fitzgerald* had begun to show the beating she was taking. The force of the storm snapped the heavy cable fencing around the deck and washed it away. The ship took a more threatening blow when the waves smashed through a pair of ventilator covers. About 3:30 P.M. Captain McSorley radioed the *Anderson* to report that he had water coming in. His vessel was operating at a list. Would the *Anderson* try to close the distance between the two ships? Yes, it would, came the reply.

Cooper had noticed no hint of desperation or even of serious concern in Captain McSorley's voice. In fact, the master of the *Fitzgerald* had given no indication at all, other than the damage reports and the request that the *Anderson* move in closer, that his ship was in trouble. Even so, Cooper resolved to keep a close watch on the *Fitzgerald.*

The blasting wind and spray and the cloak of darkness that the storm had thrown over the lake made the huge ship invisible to the unassisted eye, but its enormous hull put a substantial blip on the *Anderson*'s radar screen. In the fury of this gale, however, even radar contact was tenuous. Occasionally, an eerie thing happened: When the towering waves swelled up to block the signal, the blip representing the *Fitzgerald* would flicker and disappear from the screen.

Despite the damage, the *Fitzgerald* plowed steadily onward through the storm. Apparently, Captain McSorley was making for Whitefish Bay, where he hoped to find calmer waters. If he could round Whitefish Point and reach the bay, he might get his "Big Fitz" out of harm's way.

A lighthouse has stood on strategic Whitefish Point since 1847. In all the 150 years since, rare has been the night when sailors on the lake could not count on its powerful light for guidance. But November 10, 1975, was just such a night. The early winter storm that had whipped Lake Superior into such a pitching cauldron had also vented its rage on the shore. It ripped down road signs, uprooted trees, and even bowled over a heavily loaded tractor-trailer on the Mackinac Bridge. Among the utility poles snapped in two by the high winds was one feeding electric power to the Whitefish Point Lighthouse. And so, ironically, on the night when the *Edmund Fitzgerald* needed it the most, there was no light at Whitefish Point.

Captain McSorley put out a call to all ships in his vicinity. Could anyone see the light at Whitefish Point? McSorley got an immediate reply from the Swedish freighter *Avafors* in Whitefish Bay. The pilot of the *Avafors* reported that neither the light nor the radio beacon at Whitefish Point was operating. The pilot inquired about conditions out on the lake.

"Big sea," said McSorley. "I've never seen anything like it in my life."

Still in the relative calm and safety of the bay, the *Avafors* had not yet borne the full brunt of the storm. But that was about to change. When they ventured beyond the lee of Whitefish Point and steamed out into the lake, the crew of the *Avafors* experienced McSorley's "big sea" for themselves. Mountainous waves pounded the hull of the saltwater freighter, and winds nearing hurricane force ripped across the deck. Eventually, the *Avafors* would win its battle with the lake. Not so the *Edmund Fitzgerald*.

As the storm raged on into the evening, Captain Cooper and the crew of the *Anderson* grew increasingly worried about their compatriots aboard the *Fitzgerald*. But there had been no "Mayday"—no call for help—from the "Big Fitz," only the damage reports.

An officer on the *Anderson* radioed the *Fitzgerald*. "How are you making out?" he asked.

"We are holding our own," came the reply. Those words were the last ever heard from the *Edmund Fitzgerald*.

The men on the bridge of the *Anderson* had grown used to the wavering, ghostly radar image of the *Fitzgerald*. The sea return (radar interference caused by high waves) in this storm was tremendous. First the ship was there, then gone, then back again. Then, at some point shortly after 7:00 P.M. (no one aboard the *Anderson* ever knew exactly when), the *Edmund Fitzgerald* disappeared from the screen. And it did not return.

Minutes passed. Officers on the *Anderson* bridge checked their radar equipment. There were other ships on the screen—-upbound freighters struggling through the heavy weather. But there was no sign of the *Fitzgerald*. It was as if the giant ship, as long as a sixty-story building is tall, had slid down the side of a titanic wave and never come up again. Cooper ordered his men to try to take a visual sighting, but where the ship's running lights should have been there was only darkness. Frantic attempts to reach the *Fitzgerald* on radio were answered with silence.

Wasting no time, Captain Cooper put in a call to the Coast Guard. "No lights," he said. "Don't have her on radar. I know she's gone."

At first Cooper's report of the disappearance was met with disbelief. How could a 729-foot-long freighter vanish, and in a matter of minutes? The skepticism of his Coast Guard radio contacts must have brought a sharp response from Cooper, who had had a harrowing day. Ships' captains are legendary for their mastery of certain forms of persuasive language. No doubt Captain Cooper said what was necessary to convince the Coast Guard.

A massive search and rescue operation swung into action. Despite the savage weather, freshwater and saltwater freighters alike changed course and steamed toward the *Fitzgerald*'s last-known position. The captains and crews of these vessels were more than ready to put themselves at risk if there were any chance of saving fellow sailors perhaps even then tossing in the icy waves. Equally prepared to face the dangers of the storm were coastguardsmen, who rushed their fast cutters out onto the lake to join the search. Squadrons of aircraft, including huge C-130 transports and helicopters equipped with powerful searchlights, crisscrossed the waters off Whitefish Point. But there was no sign of the *Fitzgerald*, nor of survivors. The Whitefish Point Lighthouse, which by now was back in operation, flung its light out over a Lake Superior seemingly empty of any trace of the *Edmund Fitzgerald*. Apparently, the lake had swallowed whole the ship, cargo, and crew.

As November 11 dawned the storm abated and skies began to clear. Searchers found scattered pieces of wreckage—a propane bottle, a wooden stool, a life vest, a lifesaving ring emblazoned with the letters FITZGERALD, but very little else. The shattered remains of a wooden lifeboat turned up later in the day, and with this discovery the chances of locating anyone alive among the *Fitzgerald*'s crew of twenty-nine dwindled to nothing. Actually, there had been scarce hope of finding survivors since midnight. The surface temperature of the lake was a numbing forty-nine degrees Fahrenheit. Anyone afloat in water that cold would likely go into shock within thirty minutes and would certainly be dead within four hours.

The search went on for days, but to little effect. By the end of the week, all the crew members of the ill-fated ship were officially pronounced dead. Family, close friends, and colleagues, who had already begun their grieving, gathered in homes and chapels in Toledo, Detroit, Duluth, and other towns and cities along the shores of the Great Lakes. Church bells rang twenty-nine times as the mourners paid tribute to memories of their friends, relatives, and lovers—but not to their earthly remains. None of the bodies was ever found.

What happened? What could cause a ship the size of the *Fitzgerald* to sink so suddenly and vanish so completely? After an official inquiry convened many months after the disaster, the Coast Guard pointed a collective finger of blame at the *Fitzgerald*'s hatch covers. If they were loose or had been damaged by the storm, the high waves washing over the deck would have poured through the hatches and flooded the cargo holds. At some point, having lost critical buoyancy, the big ship would have plunged to the bottom. Another theory put forward by several of McSorley's fellow freighter captains suggests that, perhaps unknowingly, he had grazed a shoal off Caribou Island. The damage caused by striking the shoal may have led to the flooding that took the *Fitzgerald* down. Probably the most popular theory concerning the wreck maintains that a pair of towering waves raised the bow and the stern of the ship simultaneously, leaving unsupported the long center section, with its heavy cargo of iron ore. This might have caused the ship to snap in two, with the stern section rapidly following the bow to the bottom. But of course no one will ever know for sure what killed the *Fitzgerald* or what took place during those crucial moments before she went down. There were no witnesses left alive to tell the tale. According to a legend of the Ojibwa Indians, a people who have lived by the lakes for longer than even they can remember, the big lake we call Superior "never gives up the dead."

That the Ojibwa have such a legend is proof enough that they and other native peoples often ventured out onto the Great Lakes in their long canoes to fish, to trade, and to travel. No doubt they suffered calamitous wrecks of their own. The stories of those adventures, some of them tragedies, are lost in the mists of time. Or, like that of the *Edmund Fitzgerald*, they are locked away in a ghostly chamber of ice-cold water at the bottom of a lake.

LIGHTS *at the* EDGE *of an* INLAND SEA

The Ojibwa, and other ancient mariners who braved America's inland seas often turned their eyes to the sky for guidance. Sailors, no matter what seas they've sailed, have always used the night skies as a kind of celestial map. Even Captain McSorley, with all the finely calibrated compasses, radar, and other sophisticated electronic direction-finding equipment aboard the *Fitzgerald,* occasionally took a reading on the stars. But while the sailor's friend, old reliable Polaris, can point the way north, it cannot warn of a dangerous shoal, help navigate a narrow, rock-strewn channel, or mark the passage to a safe harbor. For these purposes, sailors have long looked to certain man-made "stars" along the shore.

Sailors were already braving the Earth's open waters long before the dawn of civilization. When caught in the dark, they used the faint glow of firelight from coastal encampments or villages to help them find their way to shore. The earliest maritime peoples may have banked fires on the hillsides to call their sailors home from the sea. When towns and cities grew up, lamps were placed in towers or other high places to make their harbors easier to find at night.

The world's first true lighthouse was erected about 280 B.C. at Alexandria, the old Greco–Egyptian trading center at the mouth of the Nile. It stood on an island called Pharos, near the entrance to Alexandria's bustling harbor. Towering some 450 feet above the Mediterranean Sea, it was the tallest lighthouse ever built and the one with the longest service record.

At night keepers lit bright fires at the top of the huge tower to guide Phoenicians, Greeks, Carthaginians, Romans, and other mariners from all over the known world to this fabled and prosperous city. Most came to load their ships with food grown in the Nile Delta. The rich soil of the delta was so wondrously productive that its grains fed Roman legions and city dwellers all around the Mediterranean Basin and made possible the Roman Empire. But the grain would never have reached market without the enormous lighthouse that guided sea captains and their freight ships in and out of Alexandria. The Pharos Lighthouse served faithfully for more than a thousand years until a powerful earthquake toppled it near the end of the first millennium A.D.

Like the Mediterranean of ancient times, North America's inland seas are today a heavily traveled thoroughfare. Great Lakes freighters carry an endless variety of raw materials and finished products—iron ore to steel mills, metal parts to auto assembly plants, oil and chemicals to refineries, and grain from the prodigious farms of the Midwest to hungry people all over the world.

The Great Lakes have been a key driving force in the American and Canadian economies. Long lake freighters, together with their brave crews, have fueled that engine. But the prosperity brought by commerce has come at a high price: thousands of ships sunk and many more thousands of sailors drowned or frozen to death in the lakes' dark and frigid waters.

The cost in vessels and lives would have been much higher if not for the sparkling constellation of lighthouses that ring each of the Great Lakes. For more than a century and a half, lake sailors have been guided by a linked chain of navigational lights extending more than 1,200 miles from the St. Lawrence River to Duluth. Many of the lights, such as the one at Whitefish Point in Michigan, have shined out over the lake waters since America itself was young. Most lake lighthouses are at least a century old, and some are much older. All of the lights have played an essential role in the economic development and history of the United States and Canada.

Through dramatic photographs and narrative, this book tells the story of the most historically significant and scenic lighthouses on Lakes Michigan and Superior. Travel information is included for those who wish to discover these architectural and historic treasures for themselves. If you enjoy this book, please look for our companion volume, *Eastern Great Lakes Lighthouses: Ontario, Erie, and Huron.*

Lighthouses (like the Michigan City East Pier Light, above) became the subject of one of the very first acts of Congress, in 1789, when responsibility for construction and operation of coastal lights was placed in the hands of the Treasury Department. Alexander Hamilton, whose face stares out at us from the ten-dollar bill, became the first head of the Lighthouse Service. Among Hamilton's successors was Stephen Pleasonton, a Treasury auditor who presided over the service like an Oriental satrap for nearly half a century. Pleasonton's tight-fisted stodginess delayed introduction of the advanced Fresnel lens for decades. A Lighthouse Board composed of engineers and maritime professionals replaced Pleasonton in 1852 and made rapid improvements in America's growing list of navigational lights. The board promoted widespread use of the powerful, French-made Fresnels. From 1910 until 1939 the service was governed by a separate government Bureau of Lighthouses. Then, just before World War II, responsibility for lighthouses and other navigational markers was placed entirely in the hands of the U.S. Coast Guard. Since that time many lighthouses have been discontinued, and all but one (the Boston Harbor Lighthouse) have been automated. Sadly, lighthouse keepers are now an extinct professional species in America.

Old Glory, the Michigan state flag, and the pennant of the Great Lakes Keepers Association flutter over the brick tower of the St. Helena Island Lighthouse, built in 1871. Time and weather have taken a heavy toll on the tower, now being carefully restored by the association with some energetic assistance from Michigan Boy Scouts.

CHAPTER ONE

Lights of
THE ALL-AMERICAN COAST
LAKE MICHIGAN'S EASTERN SHORE

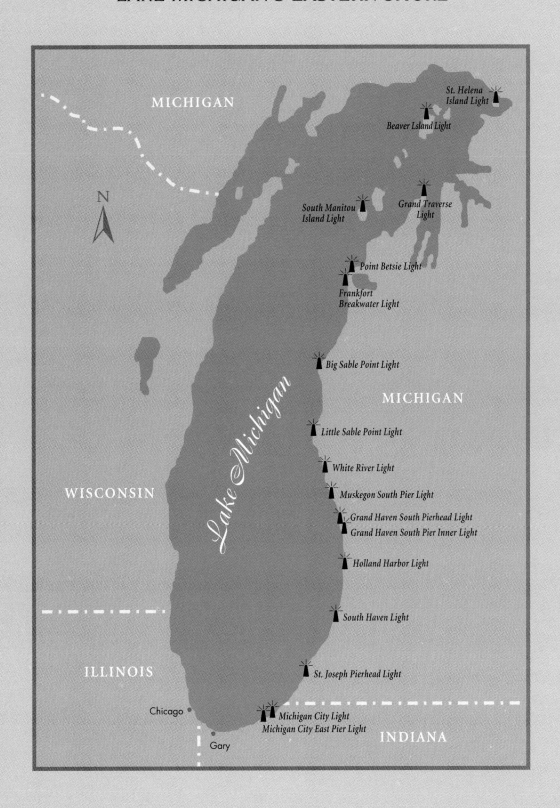

MICHIGAN

N

St. Helena
Island Light

Beaver Island Light

South Manitou
Island Light

Grand Traverse
Light

Point Betsie Light

Frankfort
Breakwater Light

Big Sable Point Light

MICHIGAN

Lake Michigan

Little Sable Point Light

White River Light

WISCONSIN

Muskegon South Pier Light

Grand Haven South Pierhead Light
Grand Haven South Pier Inner Light

Holland Harbor Light

South Haven Light

ILLINOIS

St. Joseph Pierhead Light

Chicago

Michigan City Light
Michigan City East Pier Light

Gary

INDIANA

Among the most striking of Michigan's pier lighthouses are those marking the entrance to the Grand River and one of the state's best deepwater harbors. Known as the Grand Haven South Pier Inner Light and the Grand Haven South Pierhead Light, they stand several hundred feet apart on a long stone pier. The inner light was built in 1895 and consists of a fifty-one-foot steel cylinder topped by a small lantern. The squat pierhead light was originally the fog-signal building and was moved to its current location when the pier was extended in 1905. A tiny lantern nestles on the roof. The wooden structure has been sheathed in iron to protect it from Lake Michigan's destructive, storm-driven waves.

Among the thousands of vessels lost in the Great Lakes was the very first European-style trading ship to sail their waters. In 1679 the French explorer Sieur de La Salle and a party of fur traders built a fifty-ton sailing ship, pushing it off into Lake Erie from a rough-hewn shipyard where the city of Buffalo now stands. This was no crude, overbuilt canoe. Christened the *Griffin,* it was more than sixty feet long and had five cannon arrayed below the deck. The *Griffin* was intended to make La Salle and his fellow adventurers rich by filling its holds with muskrat and beaver pelts gathered by French and Native American trappers.

The *Griffin* proved a worthy ship, weathering more than one fierce storm on the outbound leg of its maiden voyage to the far reaches of the Great Lakes. Still in 1679, La Salle disembarked to continue his explorations (while doing so, he discovered the upper Mississippi River). As he watched the *Griffin* sail away eastward, he was confident that the ship and her treasured cargo of furs would safely reach their destination. But neither the *Griffin* nor her crew was ever heard from again. Probably, like the *Fitzgerald* and so many other unlucky ships, she was smashed by a sudden, sharp autumn gale. It was an unfortunate, and ominous, beginning for commercial shipping on the Great Lakes.

THE KING *of* LAKE MICHIGAN

Over the centuries since La Salle first sailed the Great Lakes, many have traveled in his wake to Lake Michigan, seeking earthly and even heavenly rewards. One such adventurer was a Mormon outlaw named James Jesse Strang, who came to Michigan's Beaver Island during the mid-1800s and proclaimed himself king of the place. Like some religious radicals of our own time, Strang and his fervent band obeyed few earthly laws and had a penchant for violence.

Not surprisingly, Strang's non-Mormon neighbors felt threatened by his activities, which apparently included theft of supplies, weapons, and livestock. One of Strang's raiding parties even attacked the Grand Traverse Lighthouse on Cat Head, but his men were driven away by federal marshals before they could remove its Fresnel lens. Conflict was inevitable, and open warfare soon erupted, spreading throughout the Michigan islands and spilling over onto the mainland. The fighting came to an abrupt end on June 16, 1857, when Strang was gunned down by Thomas Bedford, one of his own disgruntled followers.

On June 16, 1887, thirty years to the day after her father had assassinated the "King of the Lake," Minnie Bedford boarded the steamer *Champlain* in Norwood, Michigan, for the evening run to nearby Charlevoix. The entire Strang affair, although legendary, was now far in the past, and she may or may not have considered the coincidence of the date. Whatever her thoughts at the time, Minnie Bedford was on the brink of her own Lake Michigan adventure. Instead of religious fires, however, she was about to be touched by flames of an all-too-worldly nature.

Scheduled to arrive after midnight, the *Champlain* never reached the dock in Charlevoix. As the vessel rounded Fisherman's Island, within clear sight of the harbor, fire broke out in the engine room. The fire spread quickly, blocking access to the boiler and engines, which raced crazily out of control. The *Champlain*'s increasing speed created a substantial breeze, fanning the flames and turning the ship into a giant torch. Eventually, she slammed into a shoal, throwing some of the screaming passengers overboard, while others, their clothes on fire, jumped into the water to escape the inferno. The bright flames converted the *Champlain* into a gruesome sort of lighthouse, guiding fishing boats to the scene of the disaster. In all, twenty-two of the passengers and crew drowned or were burned to death. Among the few rescued was Minnie Bedford—burned, frightened, but very much a survivor.

RAILROAD *to the* BOTTOM *of a* LAKE

In addition to the thousands of ships and boats swallowed up by Lake Michigan, more than one railroad train have gone to the bottom. Trains, or parts of them, often take an economical shortcut, crossing the lake on specially designed ferries. Some, though, never reach the tracks on the other side.

In 1910, the ferry *Pere Marquette* went down, carrying with it twenty-nine fully loaded railroad boxcars. Early on the morning of September 8, not long after leaving the terminal in Ludington, Michigan, the ferry sprung a leak. By the time a rescue ship arrived, the *Marquette* was gone, railroad cars and all. Of the sixty-two passengers and crew, only thirty-seven desperately splashing and sputtering survivors remained to be pulled from the water. The captain went down with his train.

On October 22, 1929, exactly one week before the great stockmarket crash on Wall Street, the ferry *Milwaukee* sailed out into Lake Michigan. It was never seen or heard from again. The *Milwaukee* simply vanished. Wherever she went—presumably to the bottom of the lake—she took with her twenty-seven heavily laden boxcars and at least fifty passengers, crew, and railroad men.

Huge lake freighters such as the *Edmund Fitzgerald* have been described by some as "floating trains." In fact, it would take at least three mile-long trains to carry as much iron ore as went down with her on November 10, 1975. The *Fitzgerald* was only one of many big freighters to have plied the Great Lakes' sometimes placid waters, and she was not the first of these titanic vessels to meet with disaster. In 1958, the same year that the *Fitzgerald* was launched, the lakes lost one of their biggest and proudest ships.

GONE *like the* GRIFFIN

In November 1958 the 640-foot *Carl C. Bradley* was heading home empty, making her last run of the fall shipping season. She had left behind in Buffington, Indiana, her cargo of some 18,000 tons of limestone, enough rock to fill 300 railroad cars. As the *Bradley* approached the top of Lake Michigan, less than a day's sail from her home port of Rogers City, Michigan, she ran straight into one of the lake's proverbial November storms.

Wind whipped across the deck at upwards of seventy miles per hour, and thirty-foot waves slammed into the bow. But for the *Bradley*'s thirty-five officers and crew, all hardened veterans of furious lake tempests, confronting such ugly weather was simply part of a day's work. Despite the pitching and rolling, no one got seasick as the men wolfed down their dinner of hamburgers, French fries, and sponge cake.

Groaning under the strain placed on them by the huge waves, some of the hull plates began to shear off rivets and shoot them like bullets across the empty hold. Except for anyone unlucky enough to be caught in the line of fire, this was no particular cause for alarm. It was, in fact, a common experience in a storm.

But a loud booming sound caught the attention of the entire crew just after 5:30 P.M. It was not something any of them had heard before. The boom was followed moments later by another, then another. Captain Roland Bryan and First Mate Elmer Fleming looked back from the pilothouse and, to their horror, saw the aft section of the *Bradley* begin to sag. The ship was breaking in half!

Immediately, Captain Bryan sounded a general alarm, and Fleming put out a call over the ship's radio phone to all within hearing: "Mayday! Mayday!" For the *Carl C. Bradley* and nearly all of her crew, however, it was already too late.

Less than a quarter of an hour after the first sign of trouble, the *Bradley*'s bow and stern sections parted and, within minutes, went their separate ways to the bottom. Those crewmen not carried down with the ship were left to fight for their lives on the wildly tossing surface. In those brutal, thirty-six-degree waters, it was a struggle they could not hope to win. If they could see through the storm the lighthouse beacons calling to them from nearby Beaver Island, Cat Head, or elsewhere along the Michigan coast, it must have been a bitter reminder that safe ground was so near and yet so far away. One after another of the *Bradley*'s crew froze to death or gave up and disappeared into the dark water.

The first would-be rescue ship to arrive over the *Bradley*'s watery grave was a small German freighter, the *Christian Sartori*. No survivors could be located. The *Sartori* found only an eerie scattering of wave-tossed debris. A U-boat officer in World War II, the *Sartori*'s captain Muller had witnessed such scenes in the past. He believed that all hands had been lost; but as it turned out, he was wrong. Incredibly, some fourteen hours after the big stone carrier broke in half, a Coast Guard helicopter searching the open waters of Lake Michigan spotted an orange raft. Not long afterward the crew of the cutter *Sundew* pulled aboard First Mate Fleming and Frank Mays, a young deck watchman. These two alone remained alive to tell the story of the *Carl C. Bradley*'s last day on the lake.

It is always 1920 at Raspberry Island Lighthouse. The National Park Service has furnished the keeper's house to period. This is the view from the living room; an American flag has flow from this staff since Lincoln was president.

LIGHTHOUSES OF THE MICHIGAN ISLANDS

South Manitou Island, Michigan – 1858 and 1872

Beaver Island, Michigan – 1858

St. Helena Island, Michigan – 1871

Among the most impressive structures on the Great Lakes, the South Manitou Island Light tower soars 104 feet into the skies above Lake Michigan. The stark white walls of the tower stand in sharp contrast to the beautiful natural background of the island, now included in Sleeping Bear Dunes National Lakeshore. The tower and attached keeper's dwelling were abandoned by the Coast Guard in 1958. Today they are considered part of the national lakeshore and have been handsomely restored by the U.S. Park Service.

The first lighthouse was built here in 1858 to mark the all-important Manitou Passage, frequently trafficked by ships heading to the Mackinac Straits. This early light tower was replaced by a taller lighthouse in 1858. The brick tower seen today was built in 1872. Fitted with a third-order Fresnel lens, its beacon could be seen for about eighteen miles.

The chain of islands that dot northern Lake Michigan has several other beautiful and historic lighthouses. Not particularly handsome, but certainly historic, is the North Manitou Island Shoal Lighthouse. A blocky structure built in open water directly over one of Lake Michigan's most dangerous shoals, the light has saved countless lives since it was established in 1935.

Well to the north of the Manitou Islands is Beaver Island, where the Mormon radical James Jesse Strang made his outlandish attempt to establish himself as king. He had already been deposed when the Beaver Island Lighthouse was built in 1858. Its forty-six-foot yellow-brick tower was attached to the two-story dwelling by a short passageway.

The 104-foot tower of the South Manitou Island Lighthouse soars above its colorful dwelling and outbuildings.

The Beaver Island Station was once a popular destination for sleighs ridden across the thick lake ice from Charlevoix, on the mainland. Occasionally, even cars made the trip. In 1929 three cars headed for Beaver Island got lost in a thick fog. The keeper guided them to safety with the station fog bell. Deactivated and abandoned by the Coast Guard in 1970, the lighthouse is now used as an environmental education center by local public schools.

The seventy-one-foot tower and attached dwelling built on St. Helena Island in 1871 served ships passing through the Mackinac Straits. Automated in 1922, the old station suffered from neglect and vandalism. The Great Lakes Lighthouse Keepers Association has taken on the formidable task of repairing and caring for the structure.

Boy Scouts from Michigan have been earning their Eagle Scout badges for years by helping with summer restoration work on the St. Helena Lighthouse. The isolated island offers them a rugged wilderness experience, while they, in turn, provide a service of real value to all who love lighthouses and historic architecture.

The partially restored tower of the St. Helena Island Lighthouse reaches into a Michigan blue sky.

HOW TO GET THERE:

The ferry to South Manitou Island departs from the town of Leland on the mainland. For schedules, prices, and other information, call (616) 256–9061. The South Manitou ferry passes by the North Manitou Island Shoal Lighthouse, offering a good view of the aging, but still vital, navigational light. The South Manitou Lighthouse is only a short hike from the ferry slip on the island. There are about four hours between ferries, so you have plenty of time to explore.

Beaver Island can be reached by ferry from Charlevoix. The ride takes more than three hours and can be somewhat expensive. For schedules and prices call (616) 547–2311.

St. Helena Island can be reached by boat from St. Ignace. For more information on the lighthouse and the effort to restore it, write to Great Lakes Lighthouse Keepers Association, P.O. Box 580, Allen Park, MI 48101.

Deactivated by the U.S. Coast Guard in 1970, the Beaver Island Lighthouse now serves Charlevoix County schools as an environmental-education center.

GRAND TRAVERSE LIGHT

North Port, Michigan – 1853 and 1858

Built before the Civil War, the Grand Traverse Lighthouse served several generations of lake sailors before being decommissioned in 1972. After casting its powerful beacon out across Lake Michigan for well over a century, the old lighthouse was retired, its duties taken over by a simple skeleton structure with relatively little character. But fortunately for those of us who love historic architecture, the original buildings have been preserved and are exceptionally well maintained.

Established in 1853 to guide shipping in and out of Grand Traverse Bay, the lighthouse was built on Cat Head Point. Here, with its powerful fourth-order Fresnel lens, it could command the entrance to the bay. The lens beamed out toward the lake from atop a square tower and lantern room rising through the pitched roof of a large, two-story brick dwelling. Even in this isolated location, keepers and their families could live comfortably in the ample dwelling.

The station's first keeper was Philo Beers, who also served as a U.S. deputy marshal. Apparently, the station had need of a lawman. While still under construction in 1852, it was raided by Mormon followers of a self-proclaimed king with the nearly appropriate name of Strang. Not overly literal in their reading of the Ten Commandments, these religious raiders stole everything they could lay their hands on, including some of Beers' lighthouse equipment. Fortu-

nately, the deputy marshal managed to drive off the king's men and save the station's all-important Fresnel lens.

Today the lighthouse is a museum filled with exhibits and mementos offering visitors a glimpse of life in a turn-of-the-century lighthouse. Among its exhibits is the station's original Fresnel lens.

HOW TO GET THERE:

The Grand Traverse Lighthouse is located in Leelanau State Park at the end of a long peninsula pointing northward on the Lake Michigan side of the Michigan mitten. From Traverse City follow M–22 to Northport. There you take CR–201 and follow the signs to the park. The large, two-story brick dwelling is furnished with antiques, toys, and even dishes on the table, as if the keeper and his family had just stepped outside for a moment. If you've wondered what life was like in a lighthouse, this is a good place to fuel your imagination. The lighthouse museum is open noon to 5:00 P.M. each day from the last week of June through Labor Day. In September, October, and the first three weeks of June, it is open during the same hours but on weekends only.

Lighthouse architects often combined the dwelling and tower, as they did here at Grand Traverse on Lake Michigan. This made the keeper's job a little easier. Located on Cat Head Point, the light marks the entrance of Grand Traverse Bay.

POINT BETSIE LIGHT

Frankfort, Michigan – 1858

The French called this place "Pointe Aux Becs Scies," meaning "Sawed Beak Point," but English-speaking settlers gave it a less dramatic name: Point Betsie. The government built the Point Betsie Lighthouse in 1858 to mark a key turning place for ships entering or exiting the strategic Manitou Passage. Ever since then lake sailors have considered this one of the most important lights on Lake Michigan. The original thirty-seven-foot tower and attached two-story dwelling (enlarged in 1894) still stand and the light still burns each night.

The Point Betsie Lighthouse was one of the last lights on the Great Lakes to be automated. Resident keepers operated the light until 1983, when electronic machinery took over for human hands. Coastguardsmen still live in the spacious dwelling. The tower still has its original fourth-order Fresnel lens.

For more than a century, Lake Michigan's often angry waters have chopped away at Point Betsie, eroding the beach as if determined to reclaim the land from the keepers and Coast Guard personnel. To slow the steadily advancing lake waters and save the structure, the government has erected steel breakwaters and concrete abutments. A broad concrete apron pushes out from the base of the tower to the edge of the lake. The lighthouse now seems stable enough, but in a storm you can feel the walls shake when the waves crash onto the apron.

HOW TO GET THERE:

A private residence, Point Betsie Lighthouse is closed to the public but can be viewed from the roadway. To reach Point Betsie follow M–22 for 5½ miles north from Frankfort, Michigan, and turn left onto Point Betsie Road. The road dead-ends at Lake Michigan, a little more than ½ mile ahead. The lighthouse is on the right as you approach the lake.

BIG SABLE POINT LIGHT

Ludington, Michigan – 1867 and 1924

During its early days Ludington, Michigan, had one of the most unusual fog signals in the country. A metal horn made in the shape of a long bugle, it stood beside a train track. Whenever a blanket of fog rolled in from the lake, the citizens of Ludington brought a steam locomotive up to the tongue of the horn and periodically gave a blast on its whistle. Magnified by the horn, the train whistle could be heard for many miles out on the lake.

Eventually, when lighthouse officials recognized the importance of the area to shipping, the good-hearted people of Ludington were no longer required to rely solely on their ingenuity to protect sailors out on the lake. The construction of the 107-foot-tall Big Sable Point Lighthouse just north of town in 1867 gave ships off Ludington a worthy navigational aid to guide them along the coast. The lighthouse was fitted with a third-order Fresnel lens, and a fog-signal house was built nearby.

Originally a conical brick structure, the tower had begun to crumble by the turn of the century. To save it, lighthouse officials had it encased in steel plates, giving it a ribbed appearance. The plates have done their job well—as the tower has remained solid now for nearly a century. Painted white, it has a broad black middle section to make it more distinctive as a daymark. Surrounded by shifting dunes, Big Sable is one of the more scenic light stations in the country.

HOW TO GET THERE:

To reach Big Sable Point Lighthouse, take US–10 to Ludington. Turn right onto Lakeshore Drive, follow it for approximately 6 miles, cross the Big Sable River, and enter Ludington State Park. The lighthouse can be reached only via a trail about 1/2 mile in length; but the park is so lovely, you'll be glad of the walk. You can also walk directly up the beach to the lighthouse. For directions stop at the park entrance. To get to Ludington Pierhead Lighthouse, take Ludington Avenue to Stearns Park. The lighthouse stands at the end of a long pier.

LITTLE SABLE POINT LIGHT

Silver Lake State Park, Michigan – 1874

When completed in 1874, the lighthouse tower at Little Sable Point was nearly a twin of its sister at Big Sable Point near Ludington. Both towers stood 107 feet tall, both were constructed of brick, and both had a third-order Fresnel lens.

The Big Sable Point tower deteriorated and was eventually covered with steel plates, but the tower at Little Sable Point still looks much as it did 120 years ago. The keeper's dwelling, however, was demolished during the 1950s when the lighthouse was automated, leaving the tower to stand a solitary vigil. One of the loveliest lighthouse towers on the lakes, its redbrick walls offer a handsome contrast to the white dunes and the blue water of the lake beyond.

HOW TO GET THERE:

From US–31 a few miles south of the town of Mears, turn west onto Shelby Road. After about 3½ miles turn right onto Scenic Drive, right onto Buchanan Avenue, left onto Eighteenth Avenue, and left again onto Silver Lake Road. In Silver Lake State Park, you'll find a parking area near Lake Michigan and Little Sable Point Lighthouse.

For the White River Lighthouse (see page 20), turn west from US–31 onto White Lake Road (near the town of Whitehall), then turn left onto South Shore Road and right onto Murray Road. The museum here displays the station's original fourth-order Fresnel lens.

Little Sable Lighthouse stands its solitary vigil.
(Courtesy John W. Weil)

An octagonal brick tower attached to the side of a keeper's dwelling, the White River Lighthouse served from 1875 until it was decommissioned in 1941. Today it provides the perfect setting for the Great Lakes Marine Museum, open daily June through August and on weekends in May and September. The original fourth-order Fresnel lens is on display inside.

PIERHEAD LIGHTHOUSES OF LAKE MICHIGAN

St. Joseph, Michigan – 1832, 1901, and 1907

Holland, Michigan – 1936

Grand Haven, Michigan – 1895 and 1905

Muskegon, Michigan – 1903

Many Great Lakes lighthouses are built offshore and are connected to the land by long piers or catwalks. Several fine examples of this type of lighthouse can be seen along the eastern shores of Lake Michigan. Most are located within a day's drive of one another just a few miles off US–31 in western Michigan.

St. Joseph was served by one of the earliest lighthouses on Lake Michigan. That lighthouse, built in 1832, stood on a mainland bluff. It was discontinued during the 1920s and demolished in 1955. Today the city has two lights, both located on a pier. The St. Joseph North Pier Inner and Outer lighthouses form a range-light combination, guiding ships into the St. Joseph River channel. The pier lights seen today date from 1907. With their distinctive shapes—the outer is cylindrical and the inner octagonal—they are among the most beautiful man-made structures on the Great Lakes.

To the north of St. Joseph is a solo pierhead lighthouse, located on a lengthy pier in the city of South Haven. Built in 1903, the red cylindrical tower is made of steel to protect it from the weather. In sunny weather fishermen make good use of the concrete pier, but in rough weather they do not find it so inviting. Because high waves often dash right over the pier, the lighthouse is connected to the shore by an elevated catwalk.

The Holland Harbor (Black Lake) Lighthouse is covered with steel, and no wonder: Its pierhead location exposes it to a tremendous pounding during heavy weather. The building is painted red and has a black slate roof. The tower rises through the roof of what was once the keeper's dwelling. The structure as it now appears dates to 1936.

Among the most striking of Michigan's pier lighthouses are those marking the entrance to the Grand River and one of the state's best deepwater harbors. Known as the Grand Haven South Pier Inner Light and the Grand Haven South Pierhead Light, they stand several hundred feet apart on a long stone pier. The inner light was built in 1895 and consists of a fifty-one-foot steel cylinder topped by a small lantern. The squat pierhead light was originally

The St. Joseph Pier Lighthouses, shown here at sunset, were recently featured on a commemorative postage stamp.

the fog-signal building and was moved to its current location when the pier was extended in 1905. A tiny lantern nestles on the roof. The wooden structure has been sheathed in iron to protect it from Lake Michigan's destructive, storm-driven waves.

Like many pier light towers, the Muskegon South Pier Lighthouse is painted red for better daytime recognition. Built in 1903, the tower is forty-eight feet high, and its lantern holds a fourth-order Fresnel lens. At night its light guides ships in and out of Muskegon Lake.

HOW TO GET THERE:

This list follows the Lake Michigan shoreline from south to north, and all the towns mentioned are accessible from exits off US–31. St. Joseph's North Pier Lights: In St. Joseph follow Marina Drive south to Tiscornia Park. The pier is open to the public, and the park offers an excellent view of both lights. South Haven South Pier Lighthouse: In South Haven follow Phoenix Street and then Water Street to the South Beach parking area. The light can be enjoyed and photographed from a nearby public park. Holland Harbor Lighthouse: For the best view of the lighthouse, from Holland follow Ottawa Beach Road to Holland State Park, where there is plenty of parking and an excellent beach. Grand Haven Lights: From US–31 in Grand Haven, follow Franklin Avenue and South Harbor Drive to Grand Haven State Park. The pier is open to the public and is a magnet to fishermen. The park offers camping, picnicking, and plenty of swimming. Muskegon South Pier Lighthouse: In Muskegon take Lakeshore Drive or Sherman Boulevard to Beach Street and follow it to Pere Marquette Park. The pier and lighthouse are located just north of the park, which offers swimming and picnicking.

(Above) The Holland Harbor Lighthouse wears a showy coat of red paint.

(Below) The Grand Haven Lights and Lake Michigan put on an electric display.

Fog settles over the striking Muskegon South Pier tower. Pier lighthouses are often painted red to make them easier to spot from the water.

MICHIGAN CITY LIGHT

Michigan City, Indiana – 1858

Just as Kansas City, Missouri, is not in Kansas, Michigan City is not in Michigan. It is on the Lake Michigan shore a few dozen miles to the west of South Bend, Indiana. Long an important shipping point, the Michigan City Harbor has been served by a lighthouse since 1837.

The city's first lighthouse, a simple brick-and-stone tower, was replaced by a more elaborate structure in 1858. Built with wood and brick at a cost of $8,000, it had a large central gable with a squat tower and lantern room perched on the roof. Today the old Michigan City Lighthouse looks more like a schoolhouse or library than a navigational aid. Indeed, it has been out of service since 1904, when it was replaced by a nearby pier light and converted into a residence. Eventually, the Coast Guard abandoned the building, handing it over to the Michigan City Historical Society for use as a lighthouse museum.

Out of service since 1904, the Michigan City Lighthouse is now a museum.

MICHIGAN CITY EAST PIER LIGHT

Michigan City, Indiana – 1904

The Michigan City East Pier Lighthouse has guided ships in and out of the harbor since the early twentieth century. Built on a square concrete platform, the structure has a pyramidal roof. An octagonal tower thrusts through the roof, raising the focal plane of the light more than fifty feet above the lake. Like many similar pier lighthouses, this one is encased in steel to protect it from storms.

During the tremendous storm of November 1913, the keeper of the East Pier Lighthouse took refuge on the mainland throughout most of the heavy weather. For three days the waves pounded the pier and the lighthouse. When it was all over, about 200 feet of the elevated walkway connecting the lighthouse with the mainland had been destroyed. To enable the keeper to reach the lighthouse, engineers rigged up an aerial tram with a breeches buoy (a life preserver with a pantslike canvas seat). Keepers used this rather adventurous system for several months until the elevated walkway was repaired.

It is said that, during the 1920s, keeper Ralph Moore hurried his three daughters inside whenever he saw a certain speedboat roaring through the channel. "Get . . . in the house," Moore would shout. "That damn fool is coming." The particular "damn fool" the keeper had in mind was none other than Al Capone, the Chicago gangster. Capone had a house on nearby Long Beach and reached it by boat rather than drive and take a chance on being ambushed by rival bad guys.

Connected to the mainland by a catwalk, the Michigan City East Pier Lighthouse took over from its sister lighthouse on shore in 1904. In heavy weather the catwalk provided the only safe access to the tower. During the 1920s gangster Al Capone often raced past this tower in his speedboat.

HOW TO GET THERE:

Located in Washington Park off Heisman Harbor Road, the Michigan City Lighthouse is now a delightful museum. Open from noon until 4:00 P.M., it contains many interesting exhibits, including the station's fifth-order Fresnel lens, handcrafted in Paris around the turn of the century. It is a great place to watch sunsets from the beach. To get there follow US–35 to US–12 and Pine Street (one-way), then go over a bridge into Washington Park. The lighthouse is across from the Naval Armory building and has its own parking area. To reach the Michigan City East Pier Lighthouse, drive around the park to the beach parking area (there's a small parking fee here).

Lilacs lend a peaceful spring feeling to this view of Seul Choix Lighthouse on the upper Michigan Peninsula. When cold autumn winds have swept away the last flowers, the tower's powerful beacon will be a welcome sight to mariners, especially in stormy weather. It marks the only safe harbor along a particularly dangerous stretch of Lake Michigan shoreline.

CHAPTER TWO

Lights of
THE THIRD COAST
LAKE MICHIGAN'S WESTERN SHORE

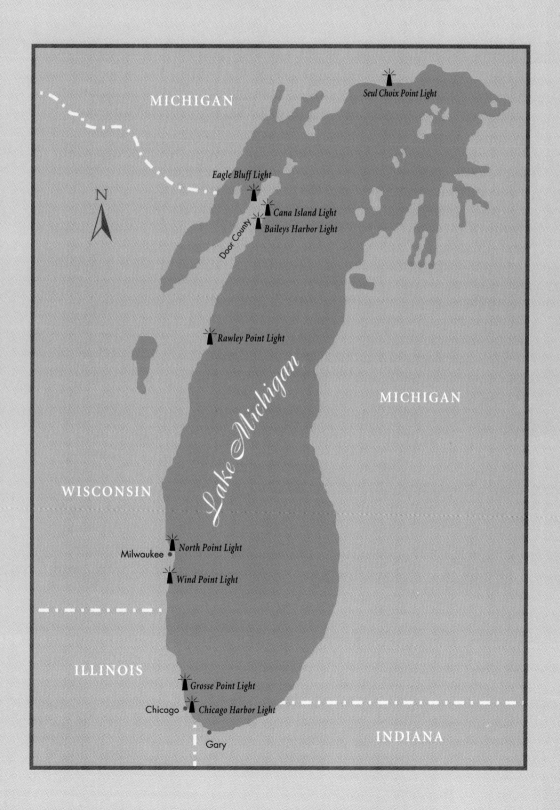

N

MICHIGAN

Seul Choix Point Light

Eagle Bluff Light

Cana Island Light

Baileys Harbor Light

Door County

Rawley Point Light

Lake Michigan

MICHIGAN

WISCONSIN

North Point Light

Milwaukee

Wind Point Light

ILLINOIS

Grosse Point Light

Chicago

Chicago Harbor Light

Gary

INDIANA

The 1874 Rawley Point Light, also known as Twin River Point, is located in Point Beach State Forest, on the west shore of Lake Michigan north of Manitowoc and Two Rivers. The tower is a marvelous combination of metal and wood, and the supporting legs cast spider-webbed shadows on the keeper's home. Now occupied by Coast Guard personnel, it and the tower are closed to the public; however, the grounds can be visited.

he entire Great Lakes region, but especially Lake Michigan and the area around Chicago, is referred to by some nowadays as the "Third Coast." This moniker, invented and played up mostly by business journalists, emphasizes the cultural and commercial likeness of the region to the Atlantic and Pacific seaboards. It also implies that this "Third Coast" has already received, or is about to inherit, the mantle of economic preeminence from the nation's "Second," or West, Coast.

The "Third Coast" distinction would have had little meaning for Lake Michigan lighthouse keepers and for the freighter captains who for nearly two centuries depended on their guidance to reach port safely. These hardy men and women were always far too busy keeping the lights burning or delivering cargoes to give much thought to fancy phrases. And with all the ships coming and going, they could hardly have helped noticing the furious pace of the industrial engine they fueled.

What is more, the similarity of the lake shores to America's storm-battered ocean coastlines was, and is, only too apparent. Like their saltwater counterparts, lake sailors fight a daily and nightly battle with wind, waves, and darkness. In fact, navigation on the lakes is even more dangerous than on the high seas. Storms strike more suddenly and often with more fury than those encountered on the open ocean; and with the lakes' limited breadth, there is very little room to maneuver, and even less for error. Without the sparkling chain of lighthouses that marked safe channels from Rochester to Duluth, the Great Lakes' economic miracle of the late nineteenth and early twentieth centuries could never have happened.

Just as lake sailors depended on lighthouse keepers, the keepers themselves depended on a small fleet of tenders to carry food, fuel, equipment, spare parts, and personnel to isolated light stations. Lighthouse tenders were usually named after flowers, trees, and shrubs. During the early decades of this century, the tender *Hyacinth*, operating out of Milwaukee and Chicago, served many of the lake lighthouses, especially those on Lake Michigan. Lighthouse keepers were always happy to see the *Hyacinth* steaming toward them with its cargo of fresh food and much-needed supplies. No doubt the lonely keepers were also glad to have visitors and enjoyed sharing news, a scrap or two of gossip, and a hot mug of coffee with the captain and crew of the *Hyacinth*.

A SEA DOG RETURNS *to the* WATER

For many years the most welcome and best-loved member of the *Hyacinth* crew was a sailor known to one and all only as "Sport." While some lake sailors may complain, rightly or wrongly, of living a dog's life, Sport never voiced such a grievance. He was, in fact, a dog who lived a sailor's life.

For more than a dozen years, Sport, a spotted mongrel, sailed with the *Hyacinth*, making friends everywhere he went. When he died of old age, he was buried in Lake Michigan with full seaman's honors. The following elegy appeared in the September 1926 *Lighthouse Bulletin* (a publication once distributed monthly by the Lighthouse Service):

To the Superintendent of Lighthouses, Milwaukee, Wisconsin

Sport was just a dog, but he was always a good dog and a good shipmate, a friend to everybody and everybody's friend. I do not think he had an enemy and I am certain that he had more friends, or perhaps I should say acquaintances, around the shores of Lake Michigan than any man on this ship today.

Sport came on board this vessel back in 1914 when engineer Albert Collins pulled him out of the Milwaukee River during a thunderstorm. He was in a pitiful condition and practically skin and bones. He was rescued and fed, and apparently, from that moment on, never had a notion to leave the ship.

Many things have happened to Sport and he has figured in many happenings aboard the ship in the 12 years he spent on board, which is longer than any officer or member of the crew has been here. It will not do to go into all the details of his life for they are many.

It is enough to say that when he was in his prime there was no place on the ship that he did not visit and nothing going on that he did not have a hand or paw in. He swam and played baseball with the boys. No boat could go ashore without Sport, and on many occasions he has carried a heaving line to shore in the breakers when landing on the beach at some light station with our crew.

He was lost in Chicago on one occasion and could not be found. We were a sad lot when we left Chicago without him and a happy lot when . . . the captain of the passenger steamer Indiana called me on the telephone to tell me he had Sport on board and to come over and get him. It was learned afterwards that someone had tied him up in a barn in Chicago, and it so happened that a man who had been a fireman on board [the Hyacinth] *was driving an ice wagon and found Sport and brought him back to our Chicago pier keeper who in turn gave him to Captain Redner on the* Indiana *to deliver to us in Milwaukee. All of which goes to show that he had friends everywhere.*

Sport died of old age on July 19, 1926. He was sewed in canvas and buried at sea the afternoon of the following day two miles off Ludington, Michigan. All hands were mustered on the spar deck where, with a few words for Sport to the effect that he had been taken from the waters and was now being returned to them, he was slid off the gangplank by a bunch of solemn-looking boys. He was given a salute and thus ended Sport, the best dog I have ever known.

Sport was not the only one pulled out of a cold river by a *Hyacinth* seaman. About the time the old sea dog took his last journey, his friends on the *Hyacinth* were making a whole series of daring rescues. In 1925 oiler Everett Wynoble jumped overboard into the freezing waters of the Chicago River to save a drowning woman. The following year in Green Bay, Wisconsin, fireman Louis Ettenhoffer performed the same service for a six-year-old boy who had fallen out of a small boat. It was early evening and Ettenhoffer was going ashore to enjoy what for him was a rare treat—a home-cooked meal at his sister's house. No sooner had his feet hit the dock than he noticed the struggling child. Ettenhoffer was himself a very poor swimmer, but he jumped into the river immediately and grabbed the boy just in time to keep him from sinking. Somehow he reached a piling and held on to it with one hand and the boy with the other until both he and the child could be rescued by other members of the *Hyacinth* crew.

In his report on the incident, the *Hyacinth*'s master, Captain H. W. Maynard, noted that "the boy had swallowed some water but was not harmed." As for Ettenhoffer, said the captain, "He had done about all the swimming he was capable of doing and had consumed a great plenty of the Fox River's water. He, however, changed his clothes and kept his dinner engagement."

Later in 1926, while tied up at a dock to service a lighthouse at Sturgeon Bay, Wisconsin, the *Hyacinth* almost became the first lighthouse tender to be hit by a car. Crewmen heard the roar of an engine and looked up in astonishment from their chores to see an automobile racing along the pier and bearing down on their ship. Luckily, the speeding car missed the *Hyacinth*; but, unfortunately for the driver, it ran right off the end of the dock into Sturgeon Bay. Although the car sank immediately, crewmen could see its lights still burning under the water. Working quickly, they managed to snare the vehicle with a grappling hook and use the tender's hoist to pull the car out of the bay.

Unhappily, their efforts were not in time to save the hapless driver. No one ever knew why he drove his car off the dock.

Even without flying cars, working on a lighthouse tender could be quite dangerous. Over the years many seamen lost their lives in the line of duty. Sailors occasionally drowned when swells overturned the small boats they used for landing passengers and supplies at remote lighthouses. Others were killed while trying to rescue the crews of wrecked ships. Some died in falls or when swept overboard by high waves. A few lost their lives while doing routine work on the tenders themselves. In 1914 seaman John Larson suffered a particularly ghastly death when a gasoline blowtorch blew up. When the fiery explosion occurred, Larson was holding the torch between his legs and using it to burn paint off the bulwarks of the tender *Marigold.*

DISASTER *on* LAKE MICHIGAN

While not so stormy as Lake Superior and not so narrow and difficult to navigate as Lake Erie, Lake Michigan has seen far more than its share of catastrophes. In fact, its list of disasters includes several of the most deadly accidents in the history of the Great Lakes. The worst among these tragedies came on the morning of July 24, 1915, less than two years after the massive storm of November 1913 and, coincidentally, only three years after the sinking of the *Titanic.* Most Great Lakes' sinkings, especially

One of several historic light stations in Wisconsin's Door County, the Cana Island Lighthouse is noted for its pristine setting. It occupies the easternmost point of a small, jewel-like island just to the east of the long, dagger-shaped peninsula separating Green Bay from Lake Michigan. This aerial view shows the clear, shallow waters surrounding the island. These same shallows pose a serious threat to shipping and were a key reason the eighty-foot light tower was erected here in 1869 only a few years after the Civil War. To reach the island today, visitors must get their feet wet by crossing a causeway (upper right) flooded by up to a foot of the lake's crystal waters.

those with a high cost in human lives, are caused by gales, collisions, or fire. But not this one. Ironically, the ship involved was still at its dock.

The sun streamed down onto the Clark Street Pier in Chicago as the steamer *Eastland* took on a heavy load of 2,500 passengers, most of them Western Electric employees and their families going on a holiday. The mood was festive, and the *Eastland*'s steam calliope kept everyone tapping their feet, clapping their hands, and singing.

The merriment continued as the gangplank came up and a tug started to pull the *Eastland* away from the dock. She moved only a few feet, however, and then began to tilt over on her port side. Someone noticed that the lines near the stern had not been released, and it was too late now to cast them off. The tug had pulled them taut, and the harder it pulled, the farther the *Eastland* tilted.

Sensing danger, the passengers panicked and crowded onto the port side, adding their enormous combined weight to the force of the tug. Soon the ship was settling into the harbor, dumping a screaming mass of humanity into the water as she went. Little more than twenty feet deep, the harbor slip was too shallow to cover the *Eastland*'s hull, but that fact did scarcely anything to lessen the plight of the struggling passengers. Thrown willy-nilly into the harbor one atop the other, most victims had little chance to save themselves. Even good swimmers were carried down in the flailing crush. When all the bodies were counted, the death toll came to an incredible 835, almost exactly a third of those on board.

A lifetime before the *Eastland* tragedy, the passenger ship *Phoenix* was destroyed by fire while crossing Lake Michigan. An estimated 250 persons died in the flames. Thirteen years later the passenger steamer *Lady Elgin* was rammed and sunk by a lumber schooner not far from Chicago. The steamer took nearly 300 passengers down with her. The accident took place in September 1860, only a couple of months before the election of President Abraham Lincoln.

While the lakes' lighthouses and their keepers could have done nothing to prevent the tragedies recounted above, they doubtlessly have saved countless ships, crews, and passengers from what might have been even worse calamities. One way that lighthouses save lives is by helping ships and their pilots keep to safe channels.

The Sherwood Point Lighthouse in Door County, Wisconsin, was not automated until 1983, making it one of the last lighthouses on the Great Lakes to have a keeper. The lighthouse is now used as a private residence by the U.S. Coast Guard and is closed to the public.

CHICAGO HARBOR LIGHT

Chicago, Illinois – 1832 and 1893

The first Chicago lighthouse, one of the earliest on the Great Lakes, was built at the mouth of the Chicago River in 1832. As Chicago grew into one of the world's greatest cities, a series of lights, built both on the mainland and on piers in the harbor, guided a tremendous volume of shipping traffic in and out of the city. Because the St. Lawrence Seaway makes Chicago a seaport and not just a lakeport, ships from every maritime nation have docked here.

The Harbor Lighthouse seen today originally stood on the mainland at the entrance of the Chicago River, near the site of the city's first lighthouse. Built in 1893, it was given an especially fine third-order Fresnel lens, which had been intended for the Point Loma Lighthouse in California. The lens had been placed on display in that same year at Chicago's Columbian Exposition. When this now-legendary world's fair was over, lighthouse officials decided to place the lens in the recently completed Harbor Lighthouse.

In 1917, just before the United States entered World War I, the lighthouse was moved to the end of a harbor breakwater. There it has remained. Each night its historic lens throws its light out across the harbor from the lantern room atop the forty-eight-foot brick-and-steel tower.

The lighthouse is closed to the public but can be seen from many points along the Chicago waterfront.

As viewed from Lake Michigan, the first spire in Chicago's well-known skyline is that of the Chicago Harbor Lighthouse. The old tower has an especially fine Fresnel lens, which was displayed at the city's 1893 Columbian Exposition. (Courtesy U.S. Coast Guard)

GROSSE POINT LIGHT

Evanston, Illinois – 1873

Among the most beautiful and storied lights on the Great Lakes, the Grosse Point Lighthouse is in many ways a superlative structure. Its second-order Fresnel is one of the most powerful lenses on the lakes, while its 113-foot tower is one of the tallest. The conical brick tower, painted yellow and trimmed in red, is exceptionally graceful.

Although it was decommissioned by the Coast Guard in 1935 and operates today as a private navigational aide, the Grosse Point Lighthouse continues to serve lake sailors just as it has since 1873. Built during the early 1870s for approximately $50,000, the station was meant to serve as a primary coastal light. It was given a double-sized keeper's dwelling and several outbuildings, which housed the fog signal and other equipment. The brick of the tower deteriorated over the years, and in 1914 the tower was encased in a layer of concrete.

Today the lighthouse stands on a street lined with fine old lakefront homes. Northwestern University is nearby. The lighthouse grounds and some of its buildings are used as a nature center and a maritime center, both open to the public on weekends during the summer. For additional information on this Evanston landmark, look for *The Grosse Point Lighthouse: Landmark to Maritime History and Culture*, a book published recently by Chicago's Windy City Press. The author, Donald Terras, has managed the Grosse Point Lighthouse Museum for more than ten years.

HOW TO GET THERE:

Take I–94 north out of Chicago or south from Milwaukee to the Old Orchard exit. Drive east toward Evanston until Old Orchard ends. Then turn left, go 2 blocks, and turn right onto Central Street. Follow Central about 4 miles until it ends at the lighthouse, which is located adjacent to Northwestern University on Sheridan Road in Evanston. The grounds are open to the public daily. Graced by stately trees almost as tall as the tower itself, the setting makes this one of the most attractive light stations on the Great Lakes. The yellow tower matches the brick of the keeper's residence. For current information call (708) 328–6961.

The elegant tower of Grosse Point Lighthouse rises far above spreading tree limbs on a quiet residential street in suburban Evanston, Illinois. The campus of Northwestern University is nearby.

WIND POINT LIGHT

Racine, Wisconsin – 1880

As early as 1866 a pier light guided ships into Racine Harbor. This arrangememt was never totally satisfactory, however, since mariners on vessels approaching from the north had their view of the harbor light blocked by Wind Point. To correct this problem, Congress appropriated $100,000 for construction of a lighthouse on the point.

Begun in 1877 and completed three years later, the Wind Point Lighthouse was fitted with a pair of lenses. Its third-order Fresnel lens displayed a flashing white light, while a smaller fifth-order lens marked the dangerous Racine Reef with a red light. Today the station is automated, and its Fresnel lens has been replaced by an airport-type beacon. The brick tower is 108 feet tall and is attached by a passageway to a two-story brick dwelling.

HOW TO GET THERE:

Follow I–94 from Milwaukee. About 2 miles south of the city limits, turn east onto CR–G. At either the first or second right, drive south to Four Mile Road. Turn east and follow Four Mile Road to Lighthouse Drive and the Wind Point Lighthouse. The town of Wind Point leases the lighthouse from the Coast Guard and uses part of the keeper's quarters for its police department. The tower and dwelling are closed to the public, but visitors may enjoy viewing the light from the spacious grounds. The Old Racine Harbor Lighthouse is closed to the public but can be seen from the pier.

The automated light atop the tall, stark white tower of the Wind Point Lighthouse still guides vessels in and out of Racine Harbor.

NORTH POINT LIGHT

Milwaukee, Wisconsin – 1855, 1888, and 1913

Milwaukee's first lighthouse, built several years before the Civil War began, served for more than thirty years before erosion threatened to topple the structure. A second tower, erected right alongside the first, was ready for service in 1888. These early towers were similar in design—octagonal in shape and made of cast iron or steel.

The 1888 tower was only thirty-five feet tall, and within two decades sprawling tree limbs began to obscure its beacon. Lighthouse engineers came up with a novel way to solve this problem in 1912. Rather than build a completely new light tower, they constructed a broad octagonal base that rose about forty feet. The old tower was then lifted on top of the base, raising its overall height to seventy-four feet. The lighthouse has served well ever since.

The lantern contains a fourth-order Fresnel lens, and its beacon helps mark the entrance to the Milwaukee River. The flashing light has a range of about twenty-one miles. The spacious keeper's dwelling adjacent to the tower is the original, dating from 1855.

The North Point Lighthouse features two octagonal towers, one perched atop the other. (Courtesy U.S. Coast Guard)

HOW TO GET THERE:

The lighthouse is located in Lake Park, just off Wahl Avenue in Milwaukee. From I–74 in downtown Milwaukee, take exit 1F and follow Lincoln Memorial Drive for 2 miles until you reach McKinley Park Beach. Instead of turning right into the beach parking area, turn left, climb the hill, and then turn right onto North Terrace Avenue. After about 1 block, turn right onto North Wahl Avenue and follow it for approximately ½ mile to the lighthouse.

LIGHTHOUSES OF DOOR COUNTY

Eagle Bluff, Wisconsin – 1868

Cana Island, Wisconsin – 1870 and 1901

Baileys Harbor, Wisconsin – 1870

During the 1860s, while the nation's attention was focused on the Civil War, shipping increased dramatically on Lake Michigan, especially along the 250-mile shoreline of Wisconsin's Door County. Native-American peoples called this land "Death's Door" because of the tricky currents and dangerous reefs that claimed the lives of so many braves who paddled their canoes through the treacherous channels into long, narrow Green Bay. European settlers who flocked here during the nineteenth century took a less foreboding view of the place and shortened the name to "Door." Not long after the influx of immigrants began, the government started building lighthouses here to make the channels less threatening. Today Door County boasts more lighthouses than any other county in the United States.

Among the earliest navigational markers established on the long, dagger-shaped peninsula that forms Green Bay was the Eagle Bluff Lighthouse. Marking a safe channel from Lake Michigan into Green Bay, its light first shined in 1868, the same year that Ulysses S. Grant was elected president. Its square, forty-three-foot brick tower was set at a diagonal into the side of the one-and-a-half-story dwelling, which made it easier for keepers to reach the tower when cold winds blew in off the lake. Ironically, there has been no keeper here since 1909. The Eagle Bluff Lighthouse was among the first in America to be automated. Still active, the old lighthouse has done its work alone for almost ninety years.

The attractive brick keeper's dwelling has been beautifully restored. The Door County Historical Society maintains a museum in the dwelling as one of the many attractions of Peninsula State Park, which also offers hiking, fishing, swimming, and golf.

At night the impressive Cana Island Lighthouse throws its beam seventeen miles out into Lake Michigan. Established in 1870, the light marks the northern approaches to Baileys Harbor. To make sure that the eighty-six-foot tower and adjacent one-and-a-half-story dwelling could withstand the lake's prodigious storms, construction crews built the structures with brick, in this case a light-colored variety. But just as a yellow-brick road may lead to an uncertain future, so too with yellow-brick lighthouses.

The Cana Island Lighthouse tower and attached dwelling were built in 1870 with the same dark yellow brick. Damaged by weather, the tower was later encased in a shell of riveted steel plates to protect it from Lake Michigan storms.

Within just a few decades, the brick showed signs of severe weathering, and the tower seemed in danger of crumbling. To protect it, the Lighthouse Board had the tower encased in a cocoonlike shell made of individual metal plates riveted together. A low, white-stone causeway connects Cana Island to the mainland.

To guide ships along the stretch of Lake Michigan nearest to Baileys Harbor, the Lighthouse Board established a pair of range lights here in 1870. These lights replaced a much older, single-lens lighthouse located on a small island far out in the harbor. Range lights mark shipping channels by displaying not one, but at least two lights, arrayed one behind the other. When viewed from mid-channel, the lights appear one atop the other and perpendicular to the surface of the water. If the lights begin to tilt to the right or left, a pilot knows that his ship may be straying dangerously out of the channel.

At Baileys Harbor the lower, or front-range, light was housed in a squat, twenty-one-foot wooden tower down beside the lake. The upper, or rear-range, light shined from a gabled tower atop a clapboard dwelling some 1,000 feet inland. The station was automated in 1930 and afterward was cared for by Lutheran ministers who used the dwelling as a parsonage right up until the lights were discontinued during the 1960s.

Door County offers at least a dozen wonderful lighthouses, most of them still active. Besides those described above, there are the Sturgeon Bay Ship Canal Lights, Potawatomi Lighthouse on Rock Island, Plum Island Range Light, Pilot Island Lighthouse, Chambers Island Lighthouse, and Sherwood Point Lighthouse. Each of these historic lighthouses has unique and interesting features, and each is well worth a visit. The best way to see and enjoy these lights is to stop first in Sturgeon Bay at the Door County Maritime Museum, located adjacent to Sunset Park at the foot of Florida Street.

Still active, the Eagle Bluff Lighthouse guides ships entering Green Bay from Lake Michigan. Note that the square tower and the dwelling were constructed from the same brick.

A tour of Door County lighthouses might well begin with the one-hundred-foot skeleton tower of the Sturgeon Bay Ship Canal Lighthouse, which features a powerful third-order Fresnel lens. The original tower, built here in 1899, was of an experimental latticework design, which proved no match for the winds blowing off the lake. The structure had to be torn down and replaced almost immediately. The tower seen today dates from 1903. This lighthouse stands on an active Coast Guard station and is off limits to the public. An excellent view can be had, however, from a nearby pier. A very interesting pierhead lighthouse stands at the end of the canal pier.

The Baileys Harbor Rear Range Lighthouse looks like a county church or schoolhouse. It once served, in fact, as a parsonage for Lutheran ministers.

HOW TO GET THERE:

To reach Eagle Bluff Lighthouse, follow Highway 42 to Fish Creek. Turn into Peninsula State Park, on the northeast side of town. Once in the park follow Lakeshore Drive about 4 miles to the lighthouse. You can buy one-hour passes for lighthouse visits at the park entrance.

To get to Cana Island Lighthouse, take Highway 57 north out of Baileys Harbor. After about 1 mile turn right onto CR–G, go 4 more miles, and turn right onto Route 38 (Cana Island Road). Follow this rustic but paved road to the end. To reach the lighthouse you must park and walk across a causeway covered by about 10 inches of water. The tower and keeper's home are not open to the public, but the view is worth getting your feet wet.

For Baileys Harbor Range lighthouses, enter Baileys Harbor on Highway 57 and turn right onto Ridges Drive. Less than a mile down the road, the Front Range Light stands on the right just a few feet off the pavement. Some 900 feet away is the Rear Range Light. Both are located on a private nature preserve, but visitors are welcome to use a path leading back to the Rear Range Light, which once served as the keeper's dwelling.

SEUL CHOIX POINT LIGHT

Gulliver, Michigan – 1895

Early French explorers found out the hard way that there were very few places to take shelter from a storm in this part of Lake Michigan. The harbor at Seul Choix was once such welcome refuge, which is why they gave it a name meaning "only choice." Despite its inviting harbor, Seul Choix Point did not receive a lighthouse until late in the nineteenth century. Congress finally appropriated the money for the project in 1886; but, partly because of its remote location, the lighthouse was not completed and fully operational until 1895.

The conical brick tower, seventy-eight feet tall, was topped by a ten-sided, cast-iron lantern, giving its third-order Fresnel lens a focal plane just over eighty feet above the lake. When the Coast Guard automated the lighthouse, the Fresnel lens was removed and replaced by an airport-style beacon, visible from about seventeen miles out in the lake.

The two-story brick keeper's dwelling still stands and is attached to the tower by an enclosed brick passageway. Although the structures and the grounds are now the property of the state of Michigan, this is still an operating light station. Neither the tower nor the dwelling is open to the public.

HOW TO GET THERE:

Turn off US–2 in the Upper Peninsula at Gulliver. Take Port Inland Road and, after about 4 miles, turn right onto CR–431 and follow it to the lighthouse. There is a small but worthy museum and gift shop in the old fog-signal building. The museum is open from noon to 4:00 P.M. every day except Sunday from mid-June until Labor Day.

Mariners on upper Lake Michigan are happy to see Seul Choix Lighthouse, looming here in the background. Feathered navigators prefer the lighthouse on the right.

CHAPTER THREE

Lights of
THE LEVIATHAN COAST

LAKE SUPERIOR'S SOUTHERN SHORE

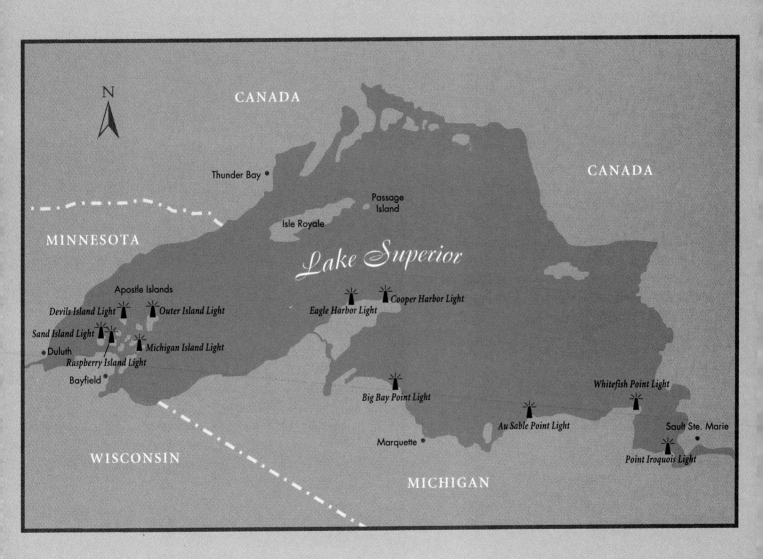

Sand Island juts out into the vastness of Lake Superior. It is one of more than twenty islands in the Apostles, named by the French, who believed there were only twelve isles here. Today the Apostle Islands invite national lakeshore visitors to enjoy an unsurpassed selection of historical lighthouses.

*K*nown to Native Americans as Gitche Gumee and to most others as Superior, it is the Earth's greatest freshwater lake. More than 350 miles long, 160 miles wide, and a quarter of a mile deep, it covers 31,200 square miles of the continental heartland in a cold, dark blanket of blue water. A liquid highway for ore, grain, and chemical freighters, container ships, and other vessels of every description, it is one of the most heavily traveled bodies of water on the planet. Yet its shores include some of the most isolated spots in North America.

Ten percent of the Earth's fresh water is locked up in this one huge lake. With the addition of a little salt, Lake Superior could be listed among the world's seas. Even without the salt, however, Superior is a mammoth body of water deserving and receiving the highest measure of respect from mariners and landlubbers alike.

Ringed by dozens of grand navigational lights, the big lake is a lighthouse lover's paradise. The Apostle Islands National Lakeshore, for instance, just off the Wisconsin mainland, boasts no fewer than seven historic lighthouses, some dating to before the Civil War and most still active. Easily accessible to visitors in summer, this well-preserved collection makes the Apostles what might be described as a "lighthouse national park." The same could be said of Michigan's Isle Royale National Park, where four magnificent light towers still guard the rocky shore.

In fact, all of Lake Superior's lighthouses are worth a visit. The lake's unmatched scenery provides a dramatic and often wilderness setting for its old lighthouses. And stories like that of the doomed passenger steamer *America,* the hapless yacht *Gunilda* (see page 73), and the *Edmund Fitzgerald* place the lights in their proper historical perspective.

THE *EDMUND FITZGERALD* REVISITED

The wreck of the *Edmund Fitzgerald* was neither the worst shipping loss nor the most mysterious disappearance on the Great Lakes. Superior has swallowed many ships. So have the other lakes. But the *Fitzgerald* has become a popular and poignant symbol for all such calamities.

In 1980 the celebrated undersea explorer Jacques Cousteau sent his famous ship *Calypso* in search of the *Fitzgerald.* The *Calypso*'s sonar located the wreck some 500 feet down, and an eager team of divers splashed into the water. The divers found a dented and misshapen hull broken into two sections. The damage they saw convinced them that the ship had broken apart on the surface. They thought that the bow and stern halves might have floated on the surface for a while before sinking. Unfortunately, Superior's ice-cold water allowed the divers only a few minutes to examine the wreck. A more careful study of the wreckage had to await the arrival of sophisticated computer technology.

During the mid-1980s computer-guided, free-swimming robots (Remote Operated Vehicles, or ROVs) made visits to the *Titanic,* the *Bismarck,* and other well-known wrecks. Oblivious to the cold, dark, and crushing pressures at extreme depths, the tireless robots could stay below for hours. In 1989 a research expedition comprising experts from the National Geographic Society, the U.S. Fish and Wildlife Service, the Great Lakes Shipwreck Historical Society, and several other organizations employed an ROV to investigate the wreck of the *Edmund Fitzgerald.* Gliding silently through an eerie world as separate from our own as the surface of the moon or Mars, the ROV turned its lights and television cameras onto the battered *Fitz.*

The data collected by the ROV led the investigators to conclude that the *Calypso*'s divers had been mistaken. Pieces of the ship had been twisted, bent, and stretched by the force of the water as the *Fitzgerald* raced, bow first, toward the bottom. Apparently, the ship had not broken up on the surface but had perished in a sudden, cataclysmic plunge into the lake's depths. We may never know what mishap—the failure of a hatch cover, the rupture of a storm-tortured hull, a collision with a shoal—sent her to the bottom.

Many other questions remain, too. The most tantalizing of them: What became of the crew? Seeking answers, the ROV headed for the *Fitzgerald*'s bridge. As the ROV worked its way carefully through the wreckage and into the pilothouse, a hush fell over the scientists on the research vessel *Grayling*, hovering way up above on the surface. What would the ROV discover?

Inside the pilothouse the ROV trained its cameras on limp microphone cables, tangled bundles of wire, a fallen watercooler, a smashed radar console, and other shattered equipment. But even here there were no clues as to the fate of the crew. Except, perhaps, for one: The port side door swung limply on its hinges. It had been left open.

Did Captain McSorley and the other men in the pilothouse escape through that open door? Did he and his crew consign themselves to the mercy of the waves only to be overwhelmed by the storm? We will never know for sure what happened to them, but guided by the light of our imaginations, perhaps we can reconstruct the final moments of the *Fitzgerald* crew.

As the last waves struck the ship, most of the men had been ordered below decks to keep them out of harm's way. To pass the time, ease the tension, and take their minds off the war that nature had declared on them and their ship, they told jokes and laughed nervously. There were stories told of other storms on other lakes, of adventures on the high seas. Some sailors' tales have roots so deep in marine tradition that they reach all the way back to the time of the Roman grain ships and before that to the age of Ulysses. The poetic memories of mariners are as ageless as the dangers they face.

Unaware that they stood on the brink of eternity, the crew of the *Fitzgerald* shared the bond that has always made brothers of sailors—and, for that matter, of lighthouse keepers. They were men caught in the grip of a hostile sea. And, as loyal sailors have always done, they counted on the keen seamanship of their captain, and a bit of luck, to pull them through.

This time their captain was not lucky. Neither were they. A shudder ran through the ship. They could feel the shudder, and hear it, while up on the bridge their captain stood peering into the darkness, searching the distance for a light.

Like spear points, limestone cliffs threaten any sailor who dares approach Devils Island in the Apostles. Because of the booming noise made by waves striking the cliffs and rushing into the caves scattered within them, Indians considered this place evil.

POINT IROQUOIS LIGHT

Brimley, Michigan – 1855 and 1871

Ships headed for the St. Marys River near Sault Ste. Marie face a pair of dangers. On their port side are the reefs near Gros Cap in Canada, while on the starboard side are the ship-killing rocks off Point Iroquois. The St. Marys became a heavily trafficked thoroughfare after the Soo Locks connected Superior to the other lakes in 1855, and since that time many vessels have been lost while approaching the river. Often an otherwise minor navigational error can be fatal here.

To help captains enter the St. Marys safely, a small lighthouse was built on Iroquois Point not long after the Soo Locks opened. Fitted with a sixth-order Fresnel lens, this modest wood tower served until 1871, when it was replaced by the impressive sixty-five-foot brick tower and dwelling that still stand on the point today. The lighthouse served for nearly a century before the Coast Guard discontinued it in 1965.

Nowadays the lighthouse is part of the Hiawatha National Forest. The structures are maintained by the Bay Mills–Brimley Historical Research Society, which operates a museum and gift shop here. Visitors get a feeling for what life was like in a nineteenth-century Great Lakes lighthouse.

Point Iroquois gets its name from a massacre that took place here in 1662. A war party sent westward by the Iroquois Confederation was set upon and slaughtered by an army of Ojibwas.

HOW TO GET THERE:

From I–75 take Highway 28 about 8 miles west to Highway 221 and the town of Brimley. From Brimley follow Six Mile Road and then Lakeshore Drive to the lighthouse. Original Lighthouse Service fixtures and equipment are on display. Rooms in the dwelling have turn-of-the-century furnishings. This lighthouse was home to Betty Byrnes Bacon, who wrote a memoir of her childhood here. Her book, Lighthouse Memories: Growing Up at Point Iroquois, is on sale at the lighthouse. For information call (906) 437–5272.

Big Bay Point Lighthouse (1896) once guarded an especially dangerous stretch of Michigan shoreline where many ships have been lost. Deactivated in 1961, Big Bay Point is now a charming bed and breakfast. Guests are welcome to climb the spiral staircase inside the five-story tower to enjoy one of the finest views in Michigan. For information call (906) 345–9957 or write to Big Bay Point Lighthouse, #3 Lighthouse Road, Big Bay, MI 49808.

WHITEFISH POINT LIGHT

Whitefish Point, Michigan – 1848 and 1861

The southeastern reaches of Lake Superior have long been known as a graveyard for ships. Hundreds of vessels, including the famed *Edmund Fitzgerald*, lay on the cold, deep bottom here where the lake approaches Whitefish Bay. The loss of so many ships in this area is made all the more bitter, and mysterious, by the fact that the bay itself is relatively calm. Seemingly, even in the worst of storms, the ships and their crews need only round Whitefish Point to reach safety. But all too often they have failed to do either.

The very first ship known to sail on Superior, the sixty-foot trading vessel *Invincible*, perished in gale-force winds and towering waves near here in 1816. Many other vessels have suffered the same fate. Some were big, well-known ships such as the *Edmund Fitzgerald,* and their destruction made headlines across the country. Many others were lesser vessels, but their loss was nonetheless tragic.

In 1915 the 186-foot lumber freighter *Myron* foundered in a blizzard off Whitefish Point. The weight of the ice building up on the hull and deck dragged the freighter farther and farther down into the waves until water, pouring into the holds, snuffed out the fires in the boiler room. With no power, the little ship was doomed. The crew managed to scramble into lifeboats, but the water around the ship was filled with tons of lumber that had washed overboard. Thrown about like battering rams by the waves, the heavy lumber crushed the lifeboats and the men in them. The keeper and his family at Whitefish Point Light Station could hear the prayers and screams of the sailors as they died, but could do nothing to help. Ironically, the captain,

A layer of fog cloaks Whitefish Point in a shroud of mystery.

who had elected to go down with his ship, survived by clinging to a piece of the shattered pilothouse until it washed up on the beach.

Probably the smallest wreck ever on Lake Superior involved no ships at all—only a surfboat and two stranded fishermen. One afternoon in April 1933, a pair of Michigan sportsmen were very unhappily surprised to discover that the field of ice where they were fishing had broken away from the mainland and drifted out onto the open lake. A Coast Guard surfboat raced out across the lake to rescue the luckless anglers. Unfortunately, the boat was caught and crushed between two massive blocks of groaning ice, leaving three coastguardsmen marooned along with the fishermen. Eventually, the keeper of Whitefish Point Light Station managed to reach the stranded men and bring them back to the lighthouse. There, no doubt, they were treated to a hot bath and warm meal.

When the November winds blow on Lake Superior, the most welcome sight a sailor is likely to see is the beacon from the Whitefish Point Lighthouse. This light has shined onto the big lake more or less unfailingly—except for the night when the *Fitzgerald* went down—for almost 150 years. To many lake sailors, the light is more than a navigational marker—it is a welcoming call from home.

The Whitefish Point Lighthouse is a remarkable structure. A steel cylinder some eighty feet tall, it is supported by a skeletal steel framework. Its modern, functional appearance is all the more extraordinary when one considers that it was built in 1861, during Abraham Lincoln's first year in the White House. Lighthouse engineers were experimenting with skeletal structures at that time. The design is intended to take stress off the building during high winds.

Storms were not the only dangers faced by lighthouses and their keepers. In February 1925 the keeper at Whitefish Bay sent this wire to officials in Detroit: "I have respectfully to report an earthquake shock being felt at this station at 8:25 last night. The shock was in the nature of a rocking and rolling and was so pronounced that the dwelling could be seen moving forth and back in an east-west direction and the window curtains swung in and out about four to six inches. Even the rocking chair in which this writer was sitting was arrested in its motion by the twisting of the dwelling. I have examined the station today, the tower in particular, and am happy to say that I can find no damage done to the lens, lantern, or the tower itself."

Automated by the Coast Guard in 1970, the station no longer has a resident keeper. Appropriately, the dwelling now houses the Great Lakes Shipwreck Museum. Here visitors with open eyes and active imaginations can step back in time and relive the last moments aboard the *Fitzgerald* and many other ill-fated ships claimed forever by the lakes.

HOW TO GET THERE:

One of America's most fabled light stations, the Whitefish Point Lighthouse can be reached from Mackinac Bridge by taking I–75 north to M–123 to Paradise. From Paradise follow Wire Road to the point. A worthwhile additional attraction is the Great Lakes Shipwreck Museum, where the haunting world of shipwrecks can be explored. The museum is open from 10:00 A.M. to 6:00 P.M. every day from Memorial Day through the middle of October.

AU SABLE POINT LIGHT

Grand Marais, Michigan – 1874

On the night of August 21, 1930, sailors aboard the lighthouse tender *Amaranth* were astonished by a mysterious beam of light cutting through the night air directly over their ship. The *Amaranth* was under way in Lake Superior about eighteen miles due west of Au Sable Point in Michigan. Barely clearing the tender's highest spars, the beam seemed about one-hundred feet wide and located directly over the ship. The light remained over the *Amaranth* for about an hour and then vanished as suddenly as it had appeared. The captain and crew of the tender were quite certain that what they saw was not an errant beam from a nearby lighthouse. Nor was it a display of the Northern Lights. Or so they reported to Lighthouse Service officials in Detroit. The strange light was never seen again, and the mystery of its appearance was never cleared up.

There are many unsolved mysteries in this part of Superior. The beaches of the Michigan Upper Peninsula are strewn with carcasses of ships large and small. What hap-

pened to these vessels? What became of their crews? Often the answers to those questions lie locked away in the lake.

For many years sailors dreaded the eighty miles of dark shoreline that stretched eastward from Grand Island Lighthouse to the famed light on Whitefish Point. Unmarked by any navigational light, these dangerous shores claimed dozens of ships. To fill the gap and save lives, a lighthouse was placed on Au Sable Point in 1874.

An eighty-seven-foot brick tower was built on a rise, placing the light about 107 feet above the lake surface. Its third-order Fresnel lens displayed a fixed white light. The attached, two-story brick keeper's dwelling was spacious, but those who lived in it knew theirs was one of the most remote mainland light stations in America. The nearest town, Grand Marais, was more than a dozen miles away, and there was no all-season road. Keepers either hiked in or came by boat.

Perhaps because of its isolation, the Coast Guard automated the light in 1958, turning the property and buildings

The lighthouse tender Amaranth *and its sister ships were the sole means of sustenance for many a grateful lighthouse keeper.* (Courtesy U.S. Coast Guard)

over to the National Park Service for inclusion in Pictured Rocks National Lakeshore. Although the light remains active, the old Fresnel lens has been removed and placed in the Nautical and Maritime Museum in Grand Marais.

Pictured Rocks National Lakeshore encompasses a remarkable variety of attractions, including Munising Falls, Miners Castle (a nine-story-tall monolith), trails, streams, woodlands, beaches, and, of course, Au Sable Light Station. Twelve miles of beach offer solitude and nearly endless barefoot walks over white sand and pebbles. Grand Sable Dunes cannot match the Sahara for sheer size, but its four square miles of shifting sand are enough to impress.

Among the least accessible mainland light stations in the United States is Au Sable Lighthouse, shown here on a sunny summer afternoon. There has never been an all-weather road to the lighthouse, and even today visitors must walk in or reach the lighthouse by means of an often treacherous dirt-and-gravel access road.

HOW TO GET THERE:

Just as its keepers once did, visitors today must walk to this lighthouse, which is located in Pictured Rocks National Lakeshore on the Upper Peninsula. From Highway 28 take Highway 77 north about 25 miles to Grand Marais. The lighthouse is a considerable distance from the park headquarters in Grand Marais. To reach it, take Alger County Road (H–58), a dirt-and-gravel access road, for about 12 miles. The Hurricane River Campground provides access to a trail leading to the lighthouse and the lake. During the summer months a ranger is on duty at the keeper's house and conducts a three-hour walk called "Shipwrecks and Lighthouses." For more information call the National Park Service at (906) 387–2607 or write to Pictured Rocks National Lakeshore, P.O. Box 40, Munising, MI 49862.

The National Park Service has established a maritime museum in a Coast Guard building in Grand Marais. Even the museum's restrooms are historic. During the November 1975 storm that sank the Edmund Fitzgerald, *the last radio contact with the ship was made from the communications room in this building. That room has been subdivided into men's and women's lavatories. A sign in each rest room says, "You are now seated in almost the same spot where the last message from the* Fitzgerald *was received."*

LIGHTHOUSES OF THE KEWEENAW PENINSULA

Copper Harbor, Michigan – 1849 and 1869

Eagle Harbor, Michigan – 1851 and 1871

The fresh water of the Great Lakes freezes more easily than the salty ocean. Beginning usually about the middle of December, winter temperatures in the frigid Upper Midwest turn lake surfaces as hard as slate. For this reason, the ice-locked lakes are closed to navigation for several months each year. In the days before lighthouses were automated, keepers on the Keweenaw Peninsula and elsewhere on Lake Superior typically shut down their lights for the winter and moved to some safer and warmer place. When winter came early and hit hard, it could make the journey very difficult indeed.

On December 16, 1925, Copper Harbor Range Light keeper Charles Davis loaded his family and belongings onto a mule-drawn wagon and prepared to move them to a nearby town. Just before he left a letter arrived from the superintendent of lighthouses, ordering Davis to keep his light burning for another three days. Freighters were still out on the lake. Like most keepers, Davis took his duties very seriously. He sent his wife and family on ahead and remained behind alone to tend the light. That evening a blizzard set in, and Davis had to wear snowshoes to walk from the keeper's dwelling to his light tower. The following is excerpted from his report on the experience.

"The snow was deep and soft. The snowshoes would sink about a foot and load up with snow at every step. I was panting like a hound before . . . I reached the main light. I had it flashing at 7:05. It took me until 8:10 to get back here. Mr. Bergh [a friend from a nearby village] had a fire started when I got back, which was a blessing as I was wringing wet with perspiration and too tired to eat, sleep, or move."

Winters on Michigan's Upper Peninsula are notoriously severe. But the weather did not deter the rapid development of mining when deposits of copper were found during the 1840s and then iron later in the century. The richest veins of copper were located on the Keweenaw Peninsula, which thrusts out to the northeast toward the center of Lake Superior. Ship traffic in and out of Copper Harbor and nearby Eagle Harbor expanded rapidly to carry the copper bounty to markets in the east.

The Copper Harbor Lighthouse has served ore freighters and other vessels since 1849. Ferry passengers can get this close-up view.

As a result, government officials soon saw the need for lighthouses at both locations.

The first Copper Harbor lighthouse was completed in 1849. A stone tower with a detached dwelling, it was located on a point near the harbor entrance. Upgraded and given a Fresnel lens in 1856, it was replaced with an entirely new structure shortly after the Civil War. A square stone tower with a small attached dwelling, this second Copper Harbor lighthouse still stands, although its duties have been taken over by a nearby skeleton tower. Copper Harbor also has a pair of range lights marking the shipping channel. The wooden rear-range lighthouse dates to 1869.

The Eagle Harbor Lighthouse, also located on Keweenaw Peninsula, began operation in 1851. During its first few years of service, it was equipped with an old-style lamp and reflector, but this outdated system was replaced by a Fresnel lens in 1857. Lake Superior weather took a heavy toll on the light-station buildings, and by 1870 they had to be replaced. The forty-four-foot, octagonal brick tower and attached dwelling seen at Eagle Harbor today date from 1871. For many years the tower held a fourth-order Fresnel lens, but in 1968 it was removed in favor of an airport-style beacon. The station has been automated since 1971.

HOW TO GET THERE:

Since there is no public road, the Copper Harbor Lighthouse can be reached only by water. Chartered boats are available at the Municipal Marina, just off MI–26 in Copper Harbor. For information call (906) 289–4215. The 15-minute boat ride to the light is pleasant, and the lovely setting of the brick tower and dwelling is well worth the trip. Inside the dwelling is a small museum, and nearby is one of the area's first copper mines, now fenced off to prevent accidents. To reach the Eagle Harbor Lighthouse, follow MI–26 down the Keweenaw Peninsula. Turn left toward the lake just before entering the town of Eagle Harbor.

The Eagle Harbor Lighthouse guards an especially rugged stretch of the Keweenaw Peninsula.

Eagle Harbor Light on the Keweenaw Peninsula is one of the most loved and visited lighthouses on Lake Michigan. The setting on a rocky hill gives it a storybook appearance. The Keweenaw Historical Society has restored the lighthouse to its early twentieth-century appearance and has transformed the outbuildings into a nautical museum open seven days a week from mid-June to early September. The museum interprets the right history of the lighthouse, detailing many of the shipwrecks of the area.

LIGHTHOUSES OF THE APOSTLE ISLANDS

Michigan Island, Wisconsin – 1857 and 1930

Raspberry Island, Wisconsin – 1863

Outer Island, Wisconsin – 1874

Sand Island, Wisconsin – 1881

Devils Island, Wisconsin – 1891

As anyone who has seen them is likely to agree, the Apostle Islands, off Wisconsin's Chequamegon Peninsula, are truly a national treasure. Fortunately, Congress has recognized their unique aesthetic value and has set aside twenty-one of the twenty-two islands by making them part of the Apostle Islands National Lakeshore.

Every summer the islands attract more and more visitors, who flock here to enjoy their natural beauty, wildlife, and pristine beaches. But the islands offer another extraordinary attraction as well: Strung in an elegant semicircle around the island chain is an elegant jeweled necklace of six lighthouses, all of them more than a century old and in excellent condition. Well maintained by National Park Service personnel, these venerable structures make the Apostle Islands National Lakeshore something of an outdoor lighthouse museum.

Built in 1857, Michigan Island Lighthouse is the oldest in the Apostles. Like many early lights in the upper Midwest, this one went into service not long after the Soo Locks opened Lake Superior to shipping from the other lakes. The whitewashed stucco tower and dwelling suggests a New England coastal lighthouse. The light guided ships along the eastern side of the Apostles for more than seventy years before its duties were taken over in 1930 by a skeleton-style light tower moved here from Maine. Still in operation today, this consists of a cylindrical metal tower supported by a framework of steel.

One of the oddities of the Michigan Island Lighthouse is the fact that it was built in the wrong place. The station was originally intended for nearby Long Island. No one knows who made the mistake, or why. In 1858 a second lighthouse was built on the correct site—La Pointe on Long Island. A simple wood-frame structure, it served until 1895,

A wisp of morning fog clings to Sand Island in the Apostles. A century-old, stone lighthouse marks the island's toe.

The oldest lighthouse in the Apostles, this masonry tower and attached dwelling were mistakenly built on Michigan Island in 1857. The station was intended for Long Island, several miles to the south.

In 1930, the U.S. Coast Guard deactivated the old Michigan Island Lighthouse, replacing it with this 102-foot skeleton tower moved from Schooner Ledge in Maine, where it had served since 1869.

when it was replaced by a steel tower similar to the one later seen on Michigan Island. In 1964 its fourth-order Fresnel lens gave way to an airport–style beacon displaying a flashing green light.

The Raspberry Island Lighthouse dates to the Civil War. Built on a high bank, the wood-frame tower and keeper's dwelling were completed in 1863. For almost a century its fifth-order lens shined from the lantern room in the forty-foot tower. Then, in 1957, the Coast Guard removed the light and mounted it on a pole in front of the fog-signal building.

The Michigan Island Light Station stands on a plateau nearly ninety feet above Lake Superior. Supplies are hauled up on an old-fashioned, cable-drawn tram.

For more than 120 years, ships have been guided around the Apostles by the Outer Island Lighthouse, in service since 1874. A traditional conical brick tower some eighty feet tall, it stands on a high bank, raising the focal plane of its light more than 130 feet above the lake surface. The lantern once held a third-order Fresnel lens, but nowadays it employs a plastic lens displaying a flashing white light.

On the west side of the Apostles, Sand Island Lighthouse guided ships for more than half a century—from 1881 to 1931—before it, too, was replaced by a steel skeleton tower. The original brownstone structure was leased afterward as a private residence, and it has survived the years since then intact.

Not long after the Sand Island Lighthouse went into service, its keeper was involved in a daring rescue. The following quote from the September 19, 1885, edition of the *Bayfield County* (Wisconsin) *Press* tells the story:

> *Saturday morning of last week Lighthouse keeper Lederle of Sand Island Light discovered a large boat*

(Left) Raspberry Island Lighthouse featured dual quarters with the keeper living on one side of the tower and his assistants on the other.

(Below) Ships circumnavigating the Apostles have looked to the Outer Island Lighthouse for guidance since 1874.

on fire about ten miles off that point. He immediately launched his boat and, notwithstanding the fact that it was blowing almost a gale from the southeast, set all for the burning steamer. When out several miles, he passed the captain, mate, engineer, and fireman of the ill-fated craft, who were pulling for shore in a metallic lifeboat. They informed him that the steamer had been abandoned and that the remainder of her crew, six men and one woman, were in a yawl boat and were being carried out into the lake. Mr. Lederle kept on his course and in a short time overhauled the yawl boat, the crew of which had given up all hope of reaching land, owing to the heavy sea and high wind which prevailed. They were soon transferred to the lighthouse boat and safely conveyed to shore, picking up on the return trip the occupants of the lifeboat. Mr. and Mrs. Lederle housed and fed the castaways until Sunday when they were brought [to the mainland] and on Tuesday they left for their several homes. . . . The boat was the Canadian propeller Prussia, bound light from Port Arthur on the north shore to Duluth, where she expected to load with grain for Montreal. Fire was first discovered about seven o'clock in the morning, issuing from her deck near the smokestack. The alarm was immediately given and the flames fought desperately for some time but to no effect.

A splash of summer color bedecks the tall grasses beside the brownstone Sand Island Lighthouse.

Devils Island has little in common with the infamous French penal colony of the same name. Keepers lived quite comfortably here in the light station's spacious Queen Anne–style brick dwelling. The station was so well-appointed, in fact, that it attracted a visit from President and Mrs. Calvin Coolidge in August 1928. Accompanied by a party of about fifty well-wishers, the fun-loving Coolidges enjoyed a sumptuous lunch on the station dock. Such events were rare, however, to say the least.

The work here was hard and demanded an extraordinary variety of skills—even the ability to handle a dog team.

The winter of 1924–25 closed in so fast that a gas-powered buoy had to be abandoned in Chequamegon Bay, just east of the Apostles. Before leaving his station for the season, a keeper drove a dogsled out over the solidly frozen lake, shut off the gas, and retrieved the buoy's valuable lantern.

Such heroics on the part of lighthouse keepers (not to mention dogs) are no longer seen in the Apostles. Devils Island Lighthouse, placed in operation in 1891, was the last of the Apostle Island lights to be automated. Electronic timers and other machinery took over from the last human keepers in 1978.

(Left) The second Devils Island tower, complete with a third-order Fresnel lens, was built in 1898 but not lit until 1901. The flashing red warning becomes a flashing white light during winter for shipping traffic loaded with lumber, iron ore, and stone. The last station to be automated in 1978, it is part of the protective ring of lights built by the U.S. Lighthouse Service to guide ships safely around the hazardous Apostle Islands.

(Inset) This rotating third-order Fresnel lens nearly fills the lantern room atop the Devils Island tower. Its bull's-eye focuses light into a narrow, flashing beam.

HOW TO GET THERE:

First visit the Apostle Islands National Lakeshore headquarters, in the old county courthouse in Bayfield. Here you can view an antique Fresnel lens, learn about the islands from the various interpretive exhibits, and pick up information on visiting the islands. To plan your tour write to National Lakeshore Headquarters, Chief of Interpretation, Route 1, Box 4, Bayfield, WI 54814.

The Apostle Islands Cruise Service offers a number of island trips, including an Inner Island Shuttle to Sand Island, with a 2-mile hike to the lighthouse there. Some trips take you to Raspberry Island and other islands, although they may not put you within reach of a lighthouse. For cruise information call (715) 779–3925 or (715) 779–5153.

CHAPTER FOUR

Lights of
THE FARAWAY COAST

LAKE SUPERIOR'S NORTHERN SHORE

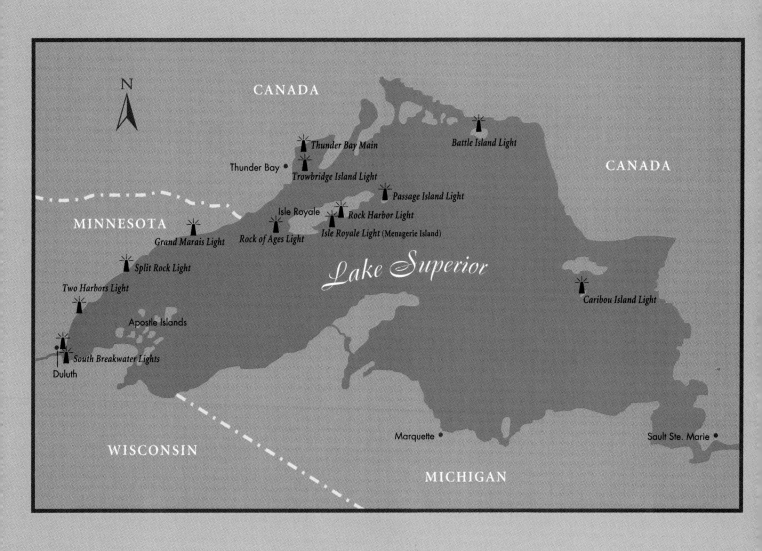

N

CANADA

Battle Island Light

CANADA

Thunder Bay Main

Thunder Bay

Trowbridge Island Light

Passage Island Light

Isle Royale

Rock Harbor Light

MINNESOTA

Grand Marais Light

Rock of Ages Light

Isle Royale Light (Menagerie Island)

Lake Superior

Split Rock Light

Caribou Island Light

Two Harbors Light

Apostle Islands

South Breakwater Lights

Duluth

Marquette

Sault Ste. Marie

WISCONSIN

MICHIGAN

An increase in traffic seeking fortunes from the newly discovered silver veins running along the rocky shores of Lake Superior brought an increase in lost vessels to the area's rocky snares and shoals. Passage Island was built in 1882 to mark the safe channel around the island's long, extended lava ridges between Thunder Bay and Isle Royale. The island has been sculpted by Earth's finest artistic tools. The result is an isolated island in a pristine archipelago, a veritable wilderness full of flora the envy of every botanical society. The clear, frigid, deep waters of Lake Superior complete the masterpiece. Passage Island remains one of the few places virtually untouched by the hand of man.

he lighthouse keepers who once served at Lake Superior's remote outposts—places like the Rock of Ages, Passage Island, Seul Choix, and Au Sable—were surely among the loneliest men and women in America, and the toughest. Usually located at water's edge, lighthouses and their keepers are often no less exposed to heavy weather than the ships and sailors they serve. But, unlike ships, lighthouses cannot move, cannot run for safe harbor, cannot remain tied up at the dock until the worst is over. In a storm they must stand their ground and take their beating, and so must their keepers.

During the 1960s and 1970s, the Coast Guard automated the last manned lighthouses on the Great Lakes, including those on Superior. Afterward, their lamps and mechanisms operated by computers, photosensitive cells, and other "electronic keepers," the lake lighthouses continued their vigil alone. In the past, however, their work had always required the help of human hands.

LIFE *on the* ROCKS

It is easy to imagine that lighthouse keepers were hermits, fugitives from noisy city streets and crowded factories who preferred a simpler, more peaceful life at water's edge. Generally speaking, however, that was not the case. Mostly they were ordinary Americans glad of the steady work and regular pay.

Keepers' salaries never amounted to much—often no more than fifty dollars per month, and much less than that during the nineteenth century; but, almost by definition, the job came with a house and an excellent view. Remote light stations were supplied with food, delivered every few months by government lighthouse tenders, and usually there was a plot of ground where the keepers could grow vegetables and raise a few chickens. Many keepers lived with their families; some stations, though, such as the Rock of Ages Lighthouse, were much too isolated or too dangerous for family life.

Looking something like an enormous spark plug, the Rock of Ages Lighthouse rises from the open waters of Lake Superior about five miles off Isle Royale, itself one of the nation's most remote places. Nowadays, like all other Great Lakes lighthouses, the Rock of Ages Light is automated. But from 1908, the year it went into service, until the last resident crew left the station in 1977, the light was operated by a keeper and three assistants, who would remain on the Rock for up to eight months at time. They arrived at the station in April and were taken ashore again in early December, when the thickening ice forced shipping off the lakes. The denizens of the Rock were allowed occasional shore leave on Isle Royale, but otherwise they lived at the station full-time. In heavy weather no one could approach the station or leave it. If radio communication went down, the station crew could be cut off from all contact with the outside world.

Utterly barren, the Rock itself was only about fifty feet wide and supported not a single bush or blade of grass. Inside the 130-foot steel-plated tower, a spiral staircase offered access to a few small bunk rooms where the keepers slept; a galley and dining area where they ate; storage and equipment rooms where they worked; and, of course, the lantern room, with its huge second-order Fresnel lens. For the most part this was the keepers' whole world.

In 1931, in the midst of the Great Depression, a young Detroit reporter named Stella Champney sailed with the tender *Marigold* as it made its semiannual visits to Lake Superior lighthouses. At the Rock of Ages Lighthouse, she interviewed first assistant keeper C. A. McKay.

This rare photograph, perhaps the only one existing, shows the lighthouse tender Marigold *making another of its appointed rounds. Named for flowers and plants, the tenders brought food, supplies, mail, and welcome human contact to keepers at isolated Great Lakes lighthouse stations.* (Courtesy Anna Hoge)

McKay had had a terrifying experience only the year before. As a storm brewed out on the lake, his boss, keeper Emil Mueller, had fallen from the tower's spiral staircase and landed squarely on the bed where McKay was sleeping. McKay was uninjured, but Mueller lay dead of a heart attack.

McKay's explanation for the tragic incident was a simple one: "Too many steps. One room on top of another clear to the top. His heart gave out."

What was it like being out here in a storm?

"You can't see anything but water," said McKay. "You can't hear anything but its roar. See that pier around the tower? It looks pretty high up and safe. Well, in a real storm, heavy, green water sweeps over it. You can't even see it sometimes. You can't get away from the water even at the top of the tower. Spray sweeps over the tower windows and, when it's very cold, freezes on the glass. You can't hear anything but the boom! boom! boom! of the seas as they sweep over the rocks, or the crack like gunfire as they hit the tower."

What about the food? McKay and some of the other men at the station complained of having to do their own cooking. "Ever hear about the time that four men nearly starved to death out here?" asked McKay. 'The tender was a week late. They had a can of tomatoes left and no tender in sight. So they piled into the lighthouse motorboat and went to the Canadian shore, more than twenty miles away, leaving a note for the skipper. He beat' em to Duluth by two days at that. They had to hunt farmhouses for food before they could work their way back to civilization."

Was it lonely living on the Rock? "You can't guess the half of it," said McKay. "No where to go on shore leave but Isle Royale. Ha! Ha!"

THE MERMAID'S SONG

The loneliness could have quite an impact on the keepers, especially those who lived without their families. Stella Champney spoke also to Passage Island keeper James Gagnon. "Live around these isolated lighthouse stations long enough and you'll be seeing mermaids," said Gagnon, "like John Whelan down at Sand Hills [Lighthouse]. He says he sees mermaids on the rocks and hears them singing." Gagnon may have thought Whelan's mermaid sightings were funny, but he was quick to add that "I'm going to hunt mermaids on Passage Island myself this summer."

Champney knew the keepers endured their loneliness and hardship for a reason. The Great Lakes—indeed, all navigable waters—are dangerous. The lights and foghorns faithfully maintained by these men, and no few women, were absolutely essential for safe navigation on stormy Lake Superior.

Not long after leaving the Rock of Ages Lighthouse, Captain Gunwald Gundersen, master of the *Marigold,* gave Champney a graphic illustration of the lake's dangers to shipping.

"That's the wreck of the Booth Fisheries steamer *America,*" Gundersen said, pointing to a ghostly bow rising from the shimmering waters off Isle Royale. "She struck a rock early one morning in the summer of 1928. She hangs over a cliff and salvage is impossible.

"I'll show you how it happened. See the perfect reflection of the trees on the water? The captain of the ship was asleep and a new mate was taking her out of the harbor. Captains must get some sleep, you know. The mate mistook the reflection on the water for land and made a miscalculation that threw him off course. The boat struck and there she lies yet. Some day she will slip off the reef and disappear forever."

Captain Gundersen assured Champney that the *America*'s "crew and the passengers got safely to shore and were taken to a hotel on Isle Royale." Both Gundersen and his guest understood, however, that many wrecks on the Great Lakes end more tragically. Less than twenty years earlier, the monster storm of November 1913 had slammed into the lakes, exacting a ghoulish toll in ships and lives. No doubt both the experienced tender captain and the young journalist who stood beside him on the bridge of the *Marigold* were all too familiar with this and many other shipping disasters on the lakes. It is easy to imagine that, as they sailed past the bow of the ruined *America,* they held their breath in a shared moment of silence.

LIGHTHOUSES OF THE DULUTH BREAKWATER

South Breakwater Lighthouses, Minnesota – 1901

At the far western angle of Lake Superior is Duluth, Minnesota, a hardworking city famous for having provided much of the iron ore fed into the Bessemer furnaces of America's steel mills. Mountains of ore have been loaded here into long Great Lakes freighters for the sometimes dangerous trip to Soo Locks and beyond. Today, in addition to freighters, the Duluth lakefront is attracting throngs of tourists.

Located in the midst of one of the nation's busiest industrial waterfronts, Canal Park offers plenty for visitors to see and enjoy. In addition to the heavily trafficked ship canal, an extraordinary aerial bridge, and a fine maritime museum, there are three delightful lighthouses, each with its own still-operational Fresnel lens.

Built just after the turn of the century, the lighthouses are located on breakwaters alongside the channel connecting the inner harbor to Lake Superior. A lighthouse was placed beside the channel as early as 1870; but in 1901 it was replaced by a pair of light towers, one at either end of the breakwater. The South Breakwater Outer Lighthouse consists of a thirty-five-foot tower rising from the corner of a squat brick fog-signal building. Its fourth-order Fresnel lens was imported from France. Erected at the same time was the South Breakwater Inner Lighthouse, a steel cylinder-type tower with a supporting skeleton frame. This lighthouse, somewhat shorter than its seaward brother, displays a flashing light produced by a fourth-order bull's-eye Fresnel lens.

The Duluth North Breakwater Lighthouse went into service during the spring of 1910. Its metal frame is enclosed by riveted steel plates. The lantern atop its thirty-seven-foot tower contains a fifth-order Fresnel lens.

HOW TO GET THERE:

From I–35 take the Highway 61 exit and follow signs to the waterfront area and Canal Park. The park is right beside the famous Aerial Bridge, only a few blocks from downtown Duluth. The lighthouses are on piers beside the ship canal. Adjacent to the canal and near the bridge is Canal Park Maritime Museum. Operated by the Army Corps of Engineers, this museum is one of the most visited attractions in Minnesota. The Duluth waterfront centers on Canal Park and is filled with busy shops and restaurants. For more information call (218) 722–4011.

TWO HARBORS LIGHT

Two Harbors, Minnesota – 1892

Looking very much like an early twentieth-century elementary school, the Two Harbors Lighthouse is not so well known as the much photographed and celebrated Split Rock Lighthouse, about twenty miles to the north. This redbrick, can-do navigational marker remains active, however, whereas its more famous neighbor is now a museum. Built in 1892 to guide iron freighters and other ships to the busy loading docks nearby, the Two Harbors Light continues to do the same job today.

Emanating from a fifty-foot square tower set into the southwest corner of the dwelling, its light has been a familiar sight to generations of lake pilots and navigators. The lighthouse sits on a grassy knoll, boosting the focal plane of the light to nearly eighty feet above the surface of the lake. The lantern room once contained a fourth-order Fresnel lens, but it was replaced with a matched pair of airport-style beacons in 1970. The Coast Guard completed automation of the lighthouse in 1981, and in 1986 it turned the building over to the Lake County Historical Society for use as a museum.

Nearby is the Two Harbors East Breakwater Lighthouse. Standing on four steel legs, it suggests an oversized metal insect in a bad science fiction movie. Despite its spindly design, the little lighthouse does its job quite efficiently, thank you. With its lantern room barely twenty-five feet above the lake, it warns sailors away from the concrete-and-stone breakwater, which could be as fatally destructive to a ship's hull as any lake shoal. Visitors are welcome to stroll out to the end of the breakwater to get an interesting perspective on both lighthouses and to enjoy a splendid view of Lake Superior.

HOW TO GET THERE:

From Highway 61 turn toward the lake on First Street, take a right onto First Avenue, and then a left onto Third Street. A parking area at the end of Third Street provides access to both lighthouses. A museum in the Two Harbors Lighthouse displays an interesting array of historical photographs and maritime equipment. The museum is open Friday and Saturday from 9:30 A.M. to 8:00 P.M., and on other days from 8:30 A.M. to 6:00 P.M. For more information on the museum and lighthouses, call (218) 834–4898.

SPLIT ROCK LIGHTHOUSE

Two Harbors, Minnesota – 1910

Compasses do not always read true in western Lake Superior. Captains steaming toward Duluth are used to seeing their compass needles swing this way and that as if the Earth's magnetic poles had decided to take a holiday. The problem is iron—mountains of it ashore and lesser mountains in the holds of passing ships. In these parts sailors are particularly thankful for lighthouses and other navigational aids.

High up on a Minnesota cliff overlooking Lake Superior stands one of the world's great lighthouses. Photographed literally millions of times, framed in countless postcards, and featured on the covers of hundreds of publications, it may be America's best-known and most visited lighthouse.

Ironically, Minnesota's Split Rock Lighthouse is no longer an official Coast Guard light station. But that does not deter the visitors who swarm here every day during the summer to enjoy this magnificent lighthouse and the spectacular view from its high, stony perch.

An octagonal yellow-brick structure, the tower is only fifty-four feet high, but the cliff beneath it soars more than 120 feet over the lake. This places the focal plane of the light 168 feet above the lake level and makes Split Rock one of the loftiest lighthouses on the Great Lakes.

Built in 1910, the lighthouse owes its existence in part to a hurricanelike November blizzard that tore across Superior five years earlier. The great Storm of 1905 caught dozens of ore boats and freighters out on the lake. More than thirty were driven onto rocks and crushed. Several disappeared forever into the lake's extreme depths. One, the 430-foot *Mataafa*, met its end within sight of Duluth Harbor. Another, the *William Edenborn*, was flung ashore and torn apart on Split Rock itself. Dozens of lives were lost in the storm.

The calamity convinced lighthouse officials that navigational aids on Lake Superior must be improved. The most important step they took to accomplish the upgrading was construction of a light station at Split Rock. Building the lighthouse proved a difficult and expensive task. Since there was no road, materials had to be shipped in and lifted to the top of the cliff, using a steam hoist. By the time the tower, lantern, fog-signal building, and detached dwellings were completed and the lamps ready to be lit, during the summer of 1910, the project had cost taxpayers more than $72,000.

The station's flashing light was produced by a bivalve-style Fresnel lens that looked something like a huge glass clamshell. For many years light for the beacon came from an oil vapor lamp; but after electricity reached the station in 1939, a 1,000-watt bulb was placed inside the lens. The light flashed once every ten seconds and could be seen from twenty-two miles out on the lake.

The fog signal was powered by gasoline or diesel compressors. Every twenty seconds during fog or heavy weather, it gave a deafening blast that could be heard from about five miles away.

The Coast Guard decommissioned the lighthouse in 1969, handing it over to the state of Minnesota for use as a park. More than 200,000 visitors enjoy the lighthouse and surrounding one hundred-acre park each year. There are several fine trails, and a variety of films and exhibits illuminate the station and its history.

HOW TO GET THERE:

Most travelers reach Split Rock from Duluth or Two Harbors via U.S. 61, otherwise known as the North Shore Highway. The park offers camping and picnicking facilities as well as trails for hiking and cross-country skiing. Accessible year-round, the park is open daily from 8:00 A.M. to 10:30 P.M. May 15 through October 15 and from 8:00 A.M. to 4:00 P.M. the rest of the year. The lighthouse, fog-signal building, keeper's dwelling, and a history center are open from 9:00 A.M. to 5:00 P.M. May 15 through October 15. The history center remains open the rest of the year, with hours from noon to 4:00 P.M. on weekends only.

A storm brews over the Split Rock Lighthouse. Mariners once looked to its powerful light for guidance in foul weather, but no more. Today this magnificent lighthouse is a popular tourist attraction.

*L*ake Superior provides a perfectly beautiful setting for the Grand Marais Lighthouse, a slightly taller
version of its sister breakwater light at Two Harbors to the south. This four-legged steel structure
stands thirty-five feet above the lake surface at the end of the Grand Marais breakwater and marks
the entrance to the harbor. The keeper's dwelling is located in the middle of town well away from the
light itself and serves as a maritime and historical museum.

THUNDER BAY MAIN LIGHT

Thunder Bay, Ontario – 1895 and 1937

Whenever a hungry person takes a bite out of a wholesome hunk of bread in Timbuktu or Kathmandu, Johannesburg or Santiago, Athens, Tel Aviv, or Bangkok, the experience may very well be linked to a little lighthouse in far-off Canada. Every year millions of tons of wheat and other grains flow from the plains of Ontario, Manitoba, Saskatchewan, and Alberta to flour mills and bakers all over the world.

Nearly every kernel is shipped to market by way of Thunder Bay, Ontario, one of the busiest grain ports on Earth. Blown into the bellies of giant freighters, the grain moves through the Great Lakes and along the St. Lawrence Seaway to Chicago, Detroit, Montreal, and hundreds of ocean ports on every continent. Marking the beginning of this epic journey is a small, boxy structure known as Thunder Bay Main Lighthouse.

Painted white and trimmed in red, the lighthouse is essentially a wooden box twenty feet on a side and thirty-one feet tall. A squat rectangular tower and a tiny lantern room sit atop the main building. Only a few small windows, some of them boarded up, grace the upper story, while diesel intake and exhaust vents push through the walls. The

Thunder Bay Lighthouse rises from the end of a harbor breakwater. The 600-foot-high cliffs of the "Sleeping Giant" can be seen in the distance.

entire structure rests on four pyramid-shaped concrete posts, which help protect it from shifting ice in winter.

Thunder Bay Main cannot be counted among Canada's most beautiful lighthouses, but its looks belie its importance. Guarding the end of a breakwater several miles long, it points the way to the open waters of mighty Lake Superior. The light makes safe passage in an out of the bustling harbor at Thunder Bay much easier, and for this reason, freighter captains and pilots from all over the world are familiar with the lighthouse and are beholden to it.

The current Thunder Bay Main Lighthouse has stood on its concrete posts since 1937, when it replaced an earlier light station built in 1895. Navigational lights and markers of one sort or another have guided mariners along this stretch of the Lake Superior shoreline since at least the early 1800s. Paddling their big canoes, French and British fur traders known as voyageurs made regular visits here during the seventeenth and eighteenth centuries. Trappers may have built signal fires to help the voyageurs find them.

In 1803 the North West Company established Fort William, near the mouth of the Kaministikwia River, as headquarters of its Lake Superior fur-trading operations. At that time North West Company trappers were locked in fierce competition with the Hudson Bay Company over dwindling stocks of beaver and other valuable pelt-bearing animals. Their rivalry grew so violent that in 1816, Hudson Bay Company officials employed an army of Swiss mercenaries to seize Fort William. The North West Company replied, predictably, with lawsuits and soldiers of its own. A few years later the two companies ended their conflict by merging. Their combined war on the North American beaver, however, soon drove the once ubiquitous dam-builders to the point of extinction, and, as the beaver disappeared, so did the fur trade.

At Fort William the old-time commerce in furs was eventually replaced by wood products and the grain grown in Canada's wondrously productive bread basket. To guide the grain freighters, a variety of small navigational lights were established in or near the harbor. Ice damaged harbor installations nearly every year, and eventually, a series of massive breakwaters was built to protect the shoreline.

The Thunder Bay Main Lighthouse stands at the end of the southernmost breakwater. The station might be known today as Port Arthur or Fort William Lighthouse, but in 1970 the two communities voted to amalgamate under the name Thunder Bay. Whatever its name, the diminutive lighthouse stands as a monument to the voyageurs of old and to the hardy folk who have chosen to make their living on the shores of Lake Superior.

On a hill only a few miles from the lighthouse is a monument of a different sort. In 1977 a Canadian athlete named Terry Fox set out from the Atlantic coast to run across Canada to raise money for cancer research. Only nineteen years old, Fox was dying from cancer himself and had already lost a leg to the disease. Incredibly, the young runner got as far as Thunder Bay before the cancer stopped him. A monument on Highway 17A marks the spot where he took the last steps of his run.

HOW TO GET THERE:

The beacon can be seen from many points along the shore. The best way to see the lighthouse, however, is from one of the harbor cruise boats operating June through early October from the Thunder Bay North Marina. To reach the marina take Highway 17 or Highway 11 to Thunder Bay, turn toward the lake on the Harbor Expressway, and then take a left onto Fort William Road. Angle right onto Water Street and then turn right onto Pearl Street. The Harbor Cruise ticket office is on the right, just past the Canadian National Railway depot. For more information on cruises, call (807) 683–8849.

Near Thunder Bay is Old Fort William, a reconstruction of the original fur-trading post. Guides dressed in period costume put the rich history of the area in perspective.

TROWBRIDGE ISLAND LIGHT

Thunder Bay, Ontario – 1910

Long before people of European ancestry arrived to build pulp mills, grain elevators, and expressways, the Ojibwa Indians came to Thunder Bay in search of peace. Tired of war with the Sioux and constant conflict with white settlers encroaching on their lands, the Ojibwa migrated from the Great Plains to the north shores of Lake Superior during the nineteenth century. According to stories still told by Ojibwa elders, they were led to the lake by Nanabijou, a giant with magical powers.

On a rocky point jutting out into the lake's cold blue waters, Nanabijou accidentally uncovered a vein of silver. Fearing that the bright metal would attract greedy people from the east and spoil the Ojibwa's idyllic refuge, Nanabijou made his tribe vow to keep the discovery a secret. Unfortunately, the Ojibwa were no strangers to greed themselves, and one of their proud chieftains made himself a set of shiny silver weapons. Word of the treasure inevitably got out, and one day a sizable party of white prospectors was seen approaching Thunder Bay in a flotilla of canoes.

To save the Ojibwa, Nanabijou called on his special powers to churn the lake into a storm and swallow up the invading prospectors. But the Great Spirit does not approve of mortal men, even of giants, who use magic

Seen here from the air, Trowbridge Island is a formidable obstacle threatening ships headed for nearby Thunder Bay.

Keepers often reached isolated Trowbridge Island by helicopter, landing on the pad at the left.

against their enemies. As a punishment, the Great Spirit turned Nanabijou to stone and lay him atop the spear of land where he had found the silver. The bold features of the "Sleeping Giant" can still seen outlined against the horizon to the east of Thunder Bay.

Perhaps less wise than the Ojibwa elders, geologists know the Sleeping Giant as Sibley Peninsula. They say it is composed of sedimentary rocks capped by an erosion-resistant igneous diabase.

The same forces that created the Sibley Peninsula, with its 600-foot-high cliffs, also placed a small island near the entrance to Thunder Bay. A few acres of rock cloaked in a dark-green blanket of pine, the island rises only about sixty feet above the surface of Lake Superior. Trowbridge Island is no giant, but standing squarely in the midst of some of the most heavily trafficked waters on Earth, it is a formidable obstacle to navigation. From a distance the island looks something like a ship itself, only this vessel remains permanently at anchor.

To help ships avoid the island and locate the harbor about fifteen miles to the west, the Canadian government launched construction of a lighthouse here during the early years of the twentieth century. Building a lighthouse on this stone citadel was no simple matter. The island is guarded on all sides by walls of rock at least fifteen feet high; this made landing materials and supplies a tricky business, especially in rough weather. Before work could begin, construction crews had to build a secure landing platform beneath the walls. Materials were then hoisted onto the island with a derrick. It was all worth the effort,

however, as the result was one of the most scenic and effective light stations in Canada.

The twenty-five-foot hexagonal wooden tower stands near the crest of the island, so the focal plane of its light reaches more than eighty feet above the lake. The ten-sided lantern room contains a fourth-order Fresnel lens, and in clear weather its light is visible from at least a dozen miles out on the lake. As with most Canadian lighthouses, the tower is painted white and trimmed in red. Located just above the landing area, a spacious keeper's dwelling with a wide porch and second-story half-dormers looks back toward Thunder Bay. A winding wooden stairway leads up to the tower.

Given the peaceful setting, extraordinary views on all sides, and the beauty of the lighthouse itself, this must have been a delightful station for keepers and their families. It was also quite isolated. During the 1970s station personnel started traveling back and forth to the island by helicopter from Thunder Bay. Today this still active and essential lighthouse has no permanent keepers. Like all other lighthouses in Canada, it has been automated.

HOW TO GET THERE:

Among Canada's most scenic light stations, Trowbridge Island Lighthouse can be reached only by boat. Its powerful beacon can be seen from several points along the coast, however. For information on cruises and other access to the light, call Welcomeship, Ltd. in Thunder Bay at (807) 683–8849.

BATTLE ISLAND LIGHT

Rossport, Ontario – 1877 and 1911

It is one of the ironies of the human condition that the filthy rich, who can most afford to be generous, are so often notorious skinflints. And sometimes their tight-fistedness costs them dearly.

This point has rarely been made with such emphasis as during the summer of 1911, when New York tycoon William L. Harkness took his palatial yacht *Gunilda* on a cruise through the Great Lakes. Along with a dozen or so pleasure-seeking guests, Harkness spent weeks exploring the far north shore of Lake Superior. No less spectacular than the wilderness scenery was the *Gunilda* herself, with her shiny brass, polished paneling, and many extravagant fineries. Throughout the trip the weather remained sunny and warm. Everyone had a perfectly delightful time, right up until the yacht turned into Nipigon Bay and steamed toward the quaint Canadian village of Rossport.

It was the morning of August 28 when assistant keeper Adolph King looked up from one of his many tasks at Battle Island Lighthouse and saw a breathtaking sight. Out picking raspberries on a barren point not far from the lighthouse, King's mother and younger brother Eli saw it, too: the sparkling white *Gunilda* steaming past Battle Island. The big yacht would have been hard to miss. Two hundred feet long, with portholes running the length of her hull and a large stack raked toward her stern, she looked more like a passenger steamer than a private yacht.

Extending into Lake Superior like a claw, these Battle Island rocks menace shipping. Even more dangerous are the nearby shoals hidden just beneath the surface—the palatial Gunilda *smashed into them in 1911. The Battle Island Lighthouse warns ships away from both obstacles.*

It was not so much her size, however, that caught the assistant keeper's attention; it was her heading. King could not understand why she would be steaming straight for McGarvey Shoal.

The explanation was a simple one, really. The wealthy Mr. Harkness had been urged to employ the services of a qualified local pilot to bring the *Gunilda* into the bay, but he flew into a rage when told he would have to pay a fifteen-dollar fee. To save himself the expense, he ordered the *Gunilda*'s captain, a man already on his payroll, to pilot her into Rossport. As it turned out, the good captain's charts were inaccurate, and he learned of McGarvey Shoal only when his beloved *Gunilda* came to a sickening, grinding halt. The yacht had been under a full head of steam, and she shoved herself so far onto the shoal that her entire bow pointed up out of the water.

Luckily, no one was seriously injured in the collision, and the vessel was in no immediate danger of sinking. The Battle Island keeper, Charlie McKay, and his assistant rowed out to the wreck to help, but there was not much they or anyone else could do. There was the *Gunilda*, firmly stuck on the shoal.

Within a day or so, the passengers had been put ashore and sent home to New York by railway. Before the week was out, Harkness had organized a salvage effort, giving him yet another opportunity to prove that his head was made of harder stuff than any Lake Superior reef.

At first the crew of the salvage tug refused to pull the *Gunilda* off the shoal, for fear she would heel over and sink. They suggested that Harkness employ at least two additional tugs to support the yacht once she was free. But again Harkness was sure he was "being taken for a ride" by the locals. "Just pull her off," he growled.

After several failed attempts the salvagers finally wrenched the *Gunilda* off the shoal. The yacht immediately heeled to starboard, put her rail in the water, and started to sink. Within minutes she was gone. For a long time Harkness and the stunned salvage crew watched the mass of rolling water and foam that marked the spot where the yacht had been, as if the *Gunilda* might suddenly pop back to the surface.

"Well," Harkness finally said with a shrug of his shoulders. "They're still building more like her."

While the Battle Island Lighthouse cannot always guard against human folly, its mission is to save freighters, yachts, and vessels of all sorts from a fate similar to that of the *Gunilda*. It has served it purpose well since 1877, when the Canadian government established the first light station here. The current concrete tower and nearby wooden dwelling date to 1911. Painted white and trimmed in red, the striking forty-three-foot octagonal tower stands at the edge of a high, black rock cliff. The combined height of the tower and cliff place the focal plane of the light almost 120 feet above the surface of the lake.

This light marks the treacherous passage into Nipigon Bay. The station was considered so important that long after most other lighthouses were automated, human eyes and hands were still thought essential here. Albert Saasto, the last lighthouse keeper on the Great Lakes, retired from his Battle Island post in 1991; however, he has remained on the island as caretaker. Now operated by switches, relays, computers, and radio signals, the Battle Island Lighthouse continues its nightly vigil. Not far away, just off McGarvey Shoal, in an ice-cold tomb more than 250 feet under the lake, the *Gunilda* sleeps, a monument to the arrogance of wealth.

HOW TO GET THERE:

Excursion cruises to Battle Island are available from Rossport Island Tours during warm weather months. For information call (807) 824–2887, (807) 767–3006, or (800) 876–2296. The lighthouse can also be viewed by private boat from the water. Rossport visitors may want to stay at the historic Rossport Inn, but since the inn has only seven rooms and a few cabins, reservations should be made well in advance at (807) 824–3213. While you are in the area, don't miss Rainbow Falls, located about 5 miles from Rossport.

Caribou Island Lighthouse guards the most dangerous shoals in the Great Lakes. Concealed just below the surface of the lake, the shoals extend out several miles from the island. Some think that they were responsible for the loss of the Edmund Fitzgerald in 1975. Captains of other ships in the vicinity on the night the Fitzgerald went down observed that she was much closer to the shoals than they themselves would like to have been. To protect mariners from the deadly shoals, a lighthouse has stood on this scrap of land just off Caribou Island since 1886. The current eighty-two-foot-tall tower, with its buttresses that give it the look of a missile gantry, has kept watch here since 1911. Because of its distance from the mainland—more than thirty miles—-access by the public to the light station is quite limited.

LIGHTHOUSES OF ISLE ROYALE

Rock Harbor – 1855

Rock of Ages – 1908

Passage Island – 1882

Isle Royale (Menagerie Island) – 1875

The state of Michigan contains one of North America's most remarkable landforms, a giant island seventy miles long and completely surrounded by the azure waters of Lake Superior. As remote as it is magnificent, Isle Royale can be seen neither from the upper nor lower Michigan peninsulas. Luckily for those of us who value wilderness and natural beauty, nearly all of the island's 209 square miles are now protected in a national park.

Today Isle Royale has the feeling of a pristine wilderness, but, surprisingly, the island was once an active mining center. The discovery of copper here during the late 1840s led to construction of the Rock Harbor Lighthouse to guide ore freighters to the island. The station included a fifty-foot brick tower with an attached stone dwelling. As it turned out the Isle Royale copper veins were exhausted within a few years, and by the late 1870s, mining activity had ceased altogether. This made the Rock Harbor Light unnecessary, and it was closed permanently in 1878. The tower and dwelling still stand.

The station's first keeper was a man named Malone, said to have been a member of the work crew that built the station. Malone was a bachelor; and when he applied for

Like a giant spark plug rising from the waters of Lake Superior, the Rock of Ages Lighthouse maintains its lonely vigil. Among the most remote light stations in North America, this isolated tower was once home to keepers who remained here for months at a time. Today the light is fully automated.

The Rock of Ages has claimed many victims, such as this rotting hulk lying just beneath the lake surface.

Isle Royale National Park provides a pristine setting for the modest tower and dwelling of Rock Harbor Lighthouse. (Courtesy Bob and Sandra Shanklin)

the position, he was told that the keeper would have to be married. Not to be undone, Malone disappeared for a month and returned with a wife in tow. He was promptly hired. This apparent marriage of convenience turned out very well indeed, as the Malones raised twelve children at the lighthouse.

When Detroit journalist Stella Champney visited Isle Royale aboard the tender *Marigold* in 1931, the Malones and their tribe had long since departed. Their story was still being celebrated, however. "The Malone children used to run and hide behind the rocks whenever the *Marigold*'s men came to the island," a sailor told Champney. "There was a new little face behind the rocks every spring."

Today there are several other lighthouses located on or near Isle Royale. Certainly, the best known of these is the Rock of Ages Lighthouse, built early in this century to mark a deadly navigational obstacle—the Rock itself. Only about 150 feet long, this exposed chunk of stone so frightened freighter captains that most favored the stormy eastern passage around Isle Royale.

To make the sheltered western passage safer and more attractive to shipping, the government undertook the herculean task of marking the Rock with a lighthouse. All materials and laborers, of course, had to be brought by ship. Construction crews first blasted an enormous hole in the stone and then built over it a massive, cylinder-shaped concrete foundation thirty feet in height. On this solid platform they constructed a 130-foot-tall tower made of steel plate and lined with brick. The project cost American taxpayers more than $138,000 in all. Some $15,000 of this went for the fine second-order Fresnel bull's-eye lens that produced the station's flashing signal.

Completed in 1908, the Rock of Ages Lighthouse was one of the most isolated manned light stations in America. Keepers had to sail more than fifty miles across the often stormy lake to spend a day in town, see a doctor, visit friends, or pick up food and supplies.

In 1933 keepers had unexpected company when the freighter *George Cox* slammed into a nearby reef. Rescued

from the lake's frigid waters, 125 survivors were crammed into the lighthouse. There they sat, one atop the other on the tower's staircase, until a ship arrived to take them to the mainland.

Anyone stranded on the Rock today, however, would find nobody at home in the lighthouse. It has been automated since 1978. The huge Fresnel lens has been replaced by a 700,000-candlepower automated beacon, the most powerful on the Great Lakes.

Located on a barren outcropping of rock at the entrance of Isle Royale's Siskit Bay, the Menagerie Island Lighthouse began operation in 1875. It was built to serve the freighter traffic that supported the local copper-mining industry. But, unlike the Rock Harbor Lighthouse, built for the same reason, the Menagerie Light is still in business. Although it has been automated since 1941, its fourth-order Fresnel lens still shines every night.

To the north of Isle Royale is Passage Island. Since 1882 the channel between the two islands has been marked by the Passage Island Light. Built high up on a cliff at the northern end of the thickly forested island, the old stone lighthouse looks out into the channel. From a distance it could, because of its architecture, be taken for a church, and for more than one sailor caught in a storm, its beacon—visible from twenty-five miles away—has been the answer to a prayer.

The isolation of Passage Island and similar remote lighthouse stations was such that keepers might not hear for weeks of a major world event or the loss of a relative. On December 7, 1925, the lighthouse superintendent in Detroit received a wire containing the sad news that the wife of Passage Island keeper Harry Thompson was dying in Marquette. The superintendent had no way to reach Thompson immediately, but he had two commercial radio stations in Detroit broadcast the unhappy news. Thompson never heard the radio reports, but the captain of a ship near Isle Royale did and stopped at Passage Island to pass on the news. As a result Thompson was able to reach Marquette in time to bid his wife farewell.

Since 1882 the Passage Island Lighthouse has marked a treacherous channel to the north of Isle Royale.
(Courtesy Bob and Sandra Shanklin)

Isolation was not the only price paid by Passage Island keepers for serving at Lake Superior's northernmost light station. Keeper James Gagnon's face and ears froze while he was sounding the fog signal for four days and three nights during a 1932 blizzard. Subzero temperatures locked much of the station in ice as Gagnon struggled continuously to keep the fog-signal machinery from freezing up. His radio signal weakened by the storm, Gagnon was unable to break through to Lighthouse Service officials in Detroit and inform them of his plight. Eventually, he managed to raise an amateur radio enthusiast on the mainland, who relayed the message to a fellow "ham" in Indianapolis, who then wired Gagnon's superiors in Detroit. Following medical treatment Gagnon was back on the job.

Storms gather over the weather-worsted Isle Royal Lighthouse. Although its dwelling was abandoned decades ago, the station's automated light still shines each evening. (Courtesy Bob and Sandra Shanklin)

HOW TO GET THERE:

The lighthouses on or near Isle Royale can be reached only by boat. Perhaps the least visited of America's national parks, Isle Royale itself is very much off the beaten path. But for wilderness lovers, and fishermen especially, a visit to this island paradise can be the experience of a lifetime. For information on transportation and facilities, write to Isle Royale National Park, 87 North Ripley Street, Houghton, MI 49931; or call (906) 482–0984. For departures from Copper Harbor, call (906) 289–4437.

BIBLIOGRAPHY

Adams, William Henry Davenport. *Lighthouses and Lightships: A Descriptive and Historical Account of Their Mode of Construction and Organization.* New York: Scribner's, 1870.

Adamson, Hans Christian. *Keepers of the Light.* New York: Greenberg, 1955.

Beaver, Patrick. *A History of Lighthouses.* Secaucus, N.J.: Citadel, 1972.

Bowen, Dana Thomas. *Shipwrecks of the Lakes.* Cleveland, Ohio: Freshwater Press, 1952.

Chase, Mary Ellen. *The Story of Lighthouses.* New York: Norton, 1965.

Havighurst, Walter. *The Great Lakes Reader.* New York: Macmillan, 1966.

Heming, Robert. *Ships Gone Missing: The Great Lakes Storm of 1913.* Chicago: Contemporary Books, 1992.

Holland, Francis Ross, Jr. *America's Lighthouses: Their Illustrated History Since 1716.* Brattleboro, Vt.: Stephen Greene Press, 1972.

———. *Great American Lighthouses.* Washington, D.C.: The Preservation Press, 1989.

Marx, Robert. *Shipwrecks of the Western Hemisphere.* New York: David McKay Company, 1971.

McCormick, William Henry. *The Modern Book of Lighthouses, Lifeboats, and Lightships.* London: W. Heinemann, 1913.

McKee, Russell. *Great Lakes Country.* New York: Crowell, 1966.

Moe, Christine. *Lighthouses and Lightships.* Monticello, Ill.: 1979.

Naush, John M. *Seamarks: Their History and Development.* London: Stanford Maritime, 1895.

Penrose, Laurie and Bill. *A Traveler's Guide to 116 Michigan Lighthouses.* Davison, Mich.: Friede Publications, 1992.

———. *A Traveler's Guide to 116 Western Great Lakes Lighthouses.* Davison, Mich.: Friede Publications, 1994.

Ratigan, William. *Great Lakes Shipwrecks and Survivals.* Grand Rapids, Mich.: Eerdmans Publishing, 1960.

Scheina, Robert L. "The Evolution of the Lighthouse Tower," *Lighthouses Then and Now.* Supplement to the U.S. Coast Guard Commandant's Bulletin.

Snowe, Edward Rowe. *Famous Lighthouses of America.* New York: Dodd, Mead, 1955.

Tinney, James and Mary Burdette-Watkins. *Seaway Trail Lighthouses: An Illustrated Guide.* Oswego, N.Y.: Seaway Trail, Inc., 1989.

United States Coast Guard. *Historically Famous Lighthouses.* CG-232, 1986.

LIGHTHOUSE INDEX

Numerals in italics indicate photograph/legend only.

FOR FURTHER INFORMATION
ON LIGHTHOUSES

Lighthouse Preservation Society
P.O. Box 736
Rockport, MA 01966

LPS is known as an advocacy group and sponsors lighthouse conferences.

Lighthouse Digest
P.O. Box 1690
Wells, ME 04090
(207) 646–0515

The *Digest* publishes an interesting monthly devoted to lighthouse news.

Great Lakes Lighthouse Keepers Association
P.O. Box 580
Allen Park, MI 48101

GLLKA publishes a quarterly journal for its members and hosts an annual meeting.

U.S. Lighthouse Society
244 Kearny Street, 5th Floor
San Francisco, CA 94108
(415) 362–7255

Members receive an interesting quarterly magazine about lighthouses, and the society conducts
worldwide tours of lighthouses.

Outer Banks Lighthouse Society
210 Gallery Row
Nag's Head, NC 27959
(919) 441–4232

Publishes an in-depth, quarterly newsletter about local lighthouses with emphasis on the keepers
and their families.

U.S. Coast Guard
Historian's Office G-CP/H
2100 2nd Street, SW
Washington, DC 20593

The Coast Guard History Office maintains operational records and historical materials related to
the U.S. Coast Guard and its predecessor agencies.

National Archives
Record Group 26
Washington, DC 20480

Record Group 26 constitutes records of the Bureau of Lighthouses and its predecessors, 1789–1939,
as well as U.S. Coast Guard records, 1828–1947, and cartographic and audiovisual materials,

1855–1963. These records are at the main archives building in Washington, D.C. Some records, such as the individual lighthouse logs, are stored at the Suitland, Maryland, branch.

Ninth Coast Guard District
1240 East 9th Street
Cleveland, OH 44199–2060

The Ninth Coast Guard District is responsible for the operation and maintenance of the lighthouses on the Great Lakes. For permission to visit lighthouses not generally open to the public, contact the public affairs officer at this address.

The Great Lakes Historical Society
480 Main Street
Vermillion, OH 44089
(216) 967–3467

The Great Lakes Historical Society maintains an extensive museum and reference library on Great Lakes maritime history, including a wealth of information on lighthouses. It is well worth the time and effort to visit here.

Shore Village Museum
104 Limerock Street
Rockland, ME 04841

The Shore Village Museum has the most extensive collection of Fresnel lenses in America. A hands-on museum, it contains hundreds of lighthouse items.

National Park Service
Maritime Initiative
P.O. Box 37127
Washington, DC 20013-7127
(2020 343–9508

The Maritime Initiative is a database that contains the most accurate information available about American lighthouses.

National Park Service
Apostle Islands National Lakeshore
Bayfield, WI 54814
(715) 779–3397

One of the best collections of American lighthouses is now under the protection of the National Park Service in the Apostle Islands.

Door County Maritime Museum
c/o Door County Hardware
244 North 3rd Avenue
Sturgeon Bay, WI 54235
(414) 743–8139

The Door County Maritime Museum is the best source of information on the fourteen lighthouses in Door County.

PHOTO INFORMATION

The pictures for this book were taken on Fuji 50 and Fuji 100 slide film. I'm sure other films would work just as well, but simplification is the only way I've survived as a professional travel photographer for the last few decades. I use only two Nikon Cameras (identical 8008s) with a small assortment of lenses. My tripod goes with me on every trip. When I was a young newspaper photographer, I thought tripods were for sissy photographers who were afraid to blur images. Now I think only fools don't use them. They ensure sharp pictures even at slow shutter speeds and give you time to compose when looking into the finder. A small Nikon flash SP-24, which fits into my camera bag, completes the equipment, except for polarizing and warming filters.

The photo of Split Rock Lighthouse on page v was taken with a 35-mm lens on the Nikon 8008 at f 5.6, 1/30 of a second on Fuji 100 film, with a polarizing filter helping enrich the color. A few seconds after this picture was taken, clouds moved in, the sunlight disappeared, and the picture was gone. I used a tripod, not to permit a slow shutter speed, but rather to hold the exact composition while waiting for waves and sunlight.

For the picture of Lee Radzak with the Fresnel lens on page viii, a 24-mm wide-angle lens was used. I was standing on the catwalk outside the lantern room shooting through the glass. I waited until the Fresnel lens was not pointing directly into the camera so that the brilliance of the light beam would not flare in the lens. The key here was to shoot after sunset, with the fading daylight in the background. The camera was hand-held at 1/30 second on Fuji 100 film, with the lens at 2.8 to let in as much light as possible.

When someone asks me how to take better lighthouse photos, I give them my thirty-second "how to" talk. First, try to arrive at the lighthouse when the light is interesting; sunrise and sunset are usually the two best times. Just before sunrise and just after sunset, there is a wonderful, soft light on most days. Sometimes clouds at these times will reflect colors and help create mood; also the lighthouse beacon may be on and add interest. Other good times may be before an approaching storm or during fog. Unusual or "bad" weather may also make good pictures.

Second, try using a telephoto lens. Because lighthouses are usually tall structures, there is the temptation to aim the camera up, which creates a "falling backward look," particularly when using wide-angle lenses. Try backing away and using a telephoto to correct the distortion. This also allows you to look for vantage points to shoot from that are overlooked by other photographers.

The picture of the moon over the Frankfort Light on the cover was taken with the 500-mm telephoto on the tripod and an exposure of about twenty seconds. I looked at my watch right after I took this, and it was 10:10 at night, almost an hour after sunset; but I was shooting west into the last bit of afterglow, which made the sky orange.

For the picture of lightning behind the Grand Haven lights on page 10, the tripod made it possible. It was more than a half-hour past sunset, and I had been waiting for the lighthouse lights to come on. Then I saw the storm coming. I stopped the lens down to f.11 and started shooting twenty-second exposures, hoping the flash of lightning would come while the shutter was open—and it did. Then I packed up and got out of there before the storm blew in.

The pictures on pages 31 and 42 of Cana Island and Sand Island were taken from a light plane. During my years of travel photography, I found that most small airports have a flying service where a plane can be rented and pilot hired by the hour, usually for under $100 for both. The more experienced pilots enjoy a photo flight, as it gives them a chance to practice their piloting skills a bit more than the usual trips. The Cessna 152 and 172 models are good because the high wing allows you to shoot down without being blocked. The window also opens. (Try to hold the lens inside the slipstream of air.) I use my 33-135-mm telephoto for these air views and always try to keep the shutter speed up at 1/250 or 1/500. The latter is better. Good pilots have slowed the plane down for me; but to stay up in the air, we have to sweep by the lighthouse at seventy to eighty miles per hour, so fast shutter speeds are the only way to get sharp pictures. My standard shutter setting is 1/500 of a second.

I have found that air views look professional if I aim down and leave out the horizon line at the top. Early morning or late afternoon is the best time for aerial photos, since the sun is low in the sky and creates shadows as the sunlight skims across the landscape.

During the day I use a polarizing filter when shooting in sunlight. It's easy to use—just rotate it around as you look through the camera and watch what happens. When the colors look their brightest, leave it there and shoot. All the sunlight shots were done with a polarizing filter. For overcast days and dusk photos (after the sun has gone below the horizon), I use a warming filter. My pick here is an 81C, which is a light brown-orange color. The photos of the Michigan City Pier Light on pages 7 and 25 needed even more color added. My maximum warming filter is a FL-D orange filter. I used it here because haze was blocking the color in the sky, making for a gray sunset. The orange filter brought the color back.

—BRUCE ROBERTS